MEDITERRANEAN DIET COOKBOOK

1500-Days Simple and Delicious 15-Min Recipes to Lose Weight and Eat Healthier Every Single Day | 28-Days Meal Plan Included

KELLY SMITH

© Copyright 2023 by   Kelly Smith - All rights reserved.

This article aims to provide accurate and trustworthy information on the subject and problem addressed. The publication is offered with the understanding that the publisher is not obligated to provide accounting services or other qualifying services that would require official authorization. If legal or professional counsel is required, a seasoned member of the profession should be contacted.

from a Declaration of Principles that two committees, one from the American Bar Association and the other from publishers and associations, accepted and endorsed equally.

Any portion of this text may not be copied, duplicated, or transmitted in any manner, whether digitally or printed. It is highly forbidden to record this publication, and the publisher must be contacted in writing before storing this material. Toutes droits réservés.

The material presented here is claimed to be accurate and reliable, with the caveat that the recipient reader bears the sole and entire risk for any misuse or inattention caused by the use of any policies, practices, or instructions included within. Under no circumstances, whether directly or indirectly, will the publisher be held liable or responsible for any compensation, damages, or monetary loss resulting from the material included herein.

All copyrights not owned by the publisher are owned by the respective authors.

The material provided here is general and is provided strictly for informative reasons. The information is presented without a contract or any sort of warranty or promise.

The trademarks are used without authorization, and the trademark owner has not given their support or approval for their publishing. All trademarks and brands mentioned in this book are used solely for the purpose of clarification and are the property of their respective owners, who are unrelated to this publication.

Table of Contents

MEDITERRANEAN DIET COOKBOOK 1
    Easy Mediterranean Diet Recipes 1
    Mediterranean Greek Orzo Salad 2
    Falafel Salad 3
    Best Ever Lentil Soup 4
    Baked Tilapia with Lemon 5
    Mediterranean Tuna Salad 6
    Moroccan Chickpea Stew 7
    Lemon Dill Salmon 8
    Quick Hummus Bowls 9
    Quinoa Stuffed Peppers Recipe 10
    Spanish Paella Recipe 11
    Tuscan Soup with White Beans 13
    Mediterranean Couscous Bowls Recipe 14
    Greek Nachos with Cilantro Sauce 15
    Best Healthy Pizza 16
    Simple Red Lentil Soup 17
    Vegetarian Tortellini Soup 18
    Easy Shakshuka with Feta 19
    Shrimp Marinara 20
    Simple Chickpea Salad 21
    Quinoa Tabbouleh 22
    Baked Shrimp with Feta and Tomatoes 23
    Easy Grilled Tilapia 24
    Greek Salad 25
    Cozy White Bean Soup 26
    Pasta e Ceci (Italian Chickpea Soup) 27
    Lentil Salad with Feta 28
    Pan Seared Scallops 29
    Easy Grain Bowl 30
    Easy Baked Shrimp 31
    Asparagus Risotto 32
    Italian Lentil Soup 33
    Best Chickpea Burgers 34
    Easy Hummus Recipe (Authentic and Homemade) 35
    Easy Sheet Pan Baked Eggs and Vegetables 36

Recipe	Page
Healthy Breakfast Egg Muffins	37
Ful Mudammas (Egyptian Fava Beans)	38
The Ultimate Mediterranean Breakfast	39
3-Ingredient Mediterranean Salad	40
10-Minute Citrus Avocado Salsa (Chunky Avocado Dip)	41
Quick Roasted Tomatoes with Garlic And Thyme	42
Roasted Cauliflower and Chickpea Stew	43
Easy White Bean Salad	44
Mediterranean Watermelon Salad Recipe	45
Traditional Greek Salad	46
Baked Zucchini with Parmesan and Thyme	47
Easy Baba Ganoush Recipe	48
Homemade Fish Sticks	49
Easy Homemade Chicken Shawarma	50
Easy Greek Red Lentil Soup	51
Easy Salmon Soup	52
Easy Authentic Falafel Recipe: Step-By-Step	53
Easy Roasted Tomato Basil Soup (Vegan, GF)	54
Black Eyed Peas Recipe (Greek Style)	55
Juicy Mediterranean-Style Salmon Burgers	56
Creamy Tahini Date Banana Shake	57
Simple Green Juice Recipe + Tips	58
Mediterranean Baked Fish Recipe with Tomatoes And Capers	59
Greek Chicken and Potatoes	60
Mediterranean-Style Sautéed Shrimp and Zucchini	61
Mediterranean Salmon Kabobs	62
Greek Shrimp with Tomatoes and Feta (Shrimp Saganaki)	63
Grilled Swordfish Recipe With A Mediterranean Twist	64
Greek Chicken Souvlaki Recipe with Tzatziki	65
Sicilian-Style Fish Stew Recipe	66
Italian-Style Sheet Pan Chicken With Vegetables	67
Mediterranean-Style Garlic Shrimp Recipe with Bell Peppers	68
Italian Baked Chicken Breast Recipe	69
One-Pan Baked Halibut Recipe With Vegetables	70
BEST Moroccan Fish Recipe	71
Baked Cod Recipe with Lemon And Garlic	72
Lebanese Rice With Vermicelli	73
Simple Vegetarian Minestrone Soup	74
BEST Mediterranean Couscous Salad	75

Simple Mushroom Barley Soup	76
Tuna Pasta Recipe, Mediterranean-Style	77
How to Cook Couscous Perfectly Every Time!	78
Mediterranean Roasted Vegetables Barley Recipe	79
Easy Moroccan Vegetable Tagine Recipe	80
Sheet-Pan Chicken Thighs with Brussels Sprouts & Gnocchi	81
Chickpea & Quinoa Bowl with Roasted Red Pepper Sauce	82
Garlic Roasted Salmon & Brussels Sprouts	83
Salmon Pita Sandwich	84
Quinoa & Chia Oatmeal Mix	85
Skillet Lemon Chicken & Potatoes with Kale	86
Fattoush Salad	87
Bourtheto Fish Stew Greek Fish Stew With Cod	88
Lemon Garlic Shrimp Pasta	89
Mushroom Chorizo and Halloumi Tacos	90
Falafel Pita Sandwich	91
Zucchini blossoms stuffed with bulgur	92
Warm spiced eggplant and chickpea salad	93
Tabbouleh	94
Louvi – Black eyed Peas	95
Greek Okra Stew Recipe with Tomatoes (Bamies Laderes)	96
Hummus	97
Grilled Swordfish with Lemon and Caper Sauce	98
Chicken Tagine with Apricots and Almonds	99
Lentil Kale Soup	100
Saffron Fish Sauce	101
Bar bunya Pinaki (Turkish Baked Beans)	102
Zesty Eggplant Frittata	103
Italian Calamari Salad	104
Greek Spinach and Rice Recipe (Spanakorizo)	105
Foraged Greens with Garlic And Paprika (Tsigarelli)	106

MEDITERRANEAN DIET COOKBOOK

Easy Mediterranean Diet Recipes

Mediterranean Greek Orzo Salad

Prep Time: 15 minutes
Cook Time: 10 minutes
Servings 8

Ingredients

- 8 ounces orzo pasta (1 ¼ cup dry)
- 1 cup canned chickpeas, drained and rinsed
- 1/2 lemon, juice and zest (about 2 tablespoons juice)
- ¼ cup minced shallot or red onion
- 1/2 English cucumber (2 cups diced, or substitute a peeled standard cucumber)
- 2 roasted red peppers from a jar or ½ fresh red bell pepper (½ cup diced)
- ⅓ cup chopped dill, plus more for garnish
- ⅓ cup chopped mint
- 2 tablespoons white wine vinegar
- 3 tablespoons extra-virgin olive oil
- ½ teaspoon Dijon mustard
- 1 teaspoon dried oregano
- ½ cup feta cheese crumbles
- ⅓ cup Kalamata olives, halved
- Black pepper

Preparation

1. Prepare the orzo according to the package instructions. Taste the orzo a few minutes before completion to ensure it's 'al dente' (chewy, but with a little firmness in the center). When it's done, drain it and then rinse it under cold water until it comes to room temperature.
2. Place the chickpeas in a bowl with the lemon zest, lemon juice, and ¼ teaspoon kosher salt.
3. Mince the red onion, then place it in a bowl with water (this helps to remove the sharp onion taste). Dice the cucumber. Dice the roasted red pepper. Chop the herbs.
4. Stir together the orzo, chickpeas and bowl of lemon juice, red onion, cucumber, red pepper, dill, mint, white wine vinegar, olive oil, Dijon mustard, oregano, feta crumbles, black olives, and several grinds of black pepper. Taste and if necessary, season with more kosher salt.

Nutritional facts

Total Fat 8.9g Saturated Fat 2.4g 10%Total Carbohydrate 28.4g 11%Dietary Fiber 3g Sugars 1.8g 14%Protein 7.2g 4%Vitamin A 33.9µg 15%Vitamin C 13.4mg 8%Calcium 108.8mg 15%Iron 2.7mg 0%Vitamin D 0.1µg 9%Magnesium 37.7mg 5%Potassium 218.8mg 17%Vitamin B6 0.3mg 7%Vitamin B12 0.2µg

Falafel Salad

Prep Time: 10 minutes
Cook Time: 25 minutes
Servings 4

Ingredients

For the baked falafel*
- 15-ounce can chickpeas
- ⅓ cup Old Fashioned rolled oats
- 1/4 small red onion
- 2 garlic cloves
- ½ cup cilantro leaves and tender stems, loosely packed (or fresh parsley)
- 2 tablespoons tahini
- 1 tablespoons olive oil
- 2 teaspoons cumin
- 1 teaspoon coriander
- ¾ teaspoon kosher salt
- Fresh ground black pepper

Preparation

1. Preheat the oven to 425 degrees Fahrenheit.
2. Drain and rinse the chickpeas. Dab the chickpeas with a paper towel to remove extra moisture and set them aside.
3. Place the rolled oats in a bowl of a food processor. Process 30 seconds to 1 minute until they are the texture of flour. Pour into a separate bowl and set aside.
4. Roughly chop the red onion and peel the garlic. Place them into the food processor with the cilantro and pulse until finely minced, stopping and scraping down the bowl once. Add the chickpeas, tahini, olive oil, cumin, coriander, salt and pepper and process until combined, stopping and scraping the bowl once. Then add the oats and pulse until a uniform dough form. (Be careful not to over-process the dough: you'll want it uniform and shape-able with a little texture. See the photo below!)
5. Line a baking sheet with parchment paper. Use your hands to roll the dough into 12 balls that are 1 ½ tablespoons each, then flatten them into discs (use a size 40 cookie scoop, if you have it). Place the discs on the baking sheet and brush the tops with olive oil.
6. Bake the falafel for 15 minutes until golden brown, then flip and bake for 10 minutes, until golden brown on the other side. Allow to cool at least 5 minutes before eating. (Storage info: The baked falafel store very well! Refrigerate up to 1 week or freeze up to 3 months. Consider making a double batch and storing leftovers.)
7. While the falafel bake, make the Tahini Dressing.
8. To serve, place greens on a plate. Top with baked falafel, shredded carrot, sliced cucumber, sliced tomato, sliced radishes, and Kalamata olives. Drizzle with tahini dressing and serve.

Nutritional fact

Total Fat 12.4g Saturated Fat 1.7g 13%Total Carbohydrate 36.4g 39%Dietary Fiber 10.9g Sugars 5g 23%Protein 11.4g 92%Vitamin A 826.8µg 36%Vitamin C 32.2mg 12%Calcium 153.9mg 24%Iron 4.4mg 0%Vitamin D 0µg 22%Magnesium 90.5mg 19%Potassium 878mg 47%Vitamin B6 0.8mg 0%Vitamin B12 0µg

Best Ever Lentil Soup

Prep Time: 10 minutes
Cook Time: 35 minutes
Servings 6

Ingredients

- 1 medium yellow onion
- 1 fennel bulb
- 2 large carrots
- 1 clove garlic
- ¼ cup olive oil
- 1 ½ cups dry brown or green lentils
- 28-ounce can dice fire roasted tomatoes
- 1-quart vegetable broth
- 1 cup water
- 1 teaspoon kosher salt
- 1 tablespoon paprika
- 1 tablespoon dried oregano
- 3 cups baby spinach (or chopped standard spinach)

Preparation

- Dice the onion. Dice the fennel. Peel and dice the carrots. Grate the garlic and set aside to stir in once the soup is cooked. (Got an Instant Pot? Go to Instant Pot Lentil Soup and continue at Step 2!)
- In a large pot, heat the olive oil over medium heat. Add the onion and fennel and saute for 6 to 7 minutes until translucent. Add the carrots, lentils, tomatoes, broth, water, salt, paprika, and oregano.
- Bring to a simmer. Simmer for 22 to 25 minutes until the lentils are tender.
- Stir in the spinach and grated garlic, and allow it to rest for 5 minutes before serving. Taste and season with additional salt and fresh ground pepper as necessary. Serve immediately. Stores refrigerated for up to 4 days and frozen for 3 to 4 months.

Nutrition fact

Total Fat 10.4g Saturated Fat 1.5g 17%Total Carbohydrate 46.7g 31%Dietary Fiber 8.7g Sugars 9.3g 28%Protein 14.2g 32%Vitamin A 287.9µg 23%Vitamin C 20.9mg 8%Calcium 105.9mg 33%Iron 5.9mg 0%Vitamin D 0µg 14%Magnesium 60.3mg18%Potassium 858.7mg n24%Vitamin B6 0.4mg 0%Vitamin B12 0µg

Baked Tilapia with Lemon

Prep Time: 10 minutes
Cook Time: 20 minutes
Servings 4

Ingredients

- 1-pint cherry tomatoes, sliced in half
- 1 large shallot, thinly sliced
- 3 garlic cloves, minced
- 1 small lemon, thinly sliced into rings
- 2 tablespoons olive oil, divided
- ¾ teaspoon kosher salt
- 4 ounce block feta cheese
- 1 1/2 pounds tilapia
- 1 tablespoon Italian seasoning
- 1 pinch red pepper flakes (optional)
- ½ teaspoon smoked paprika (or standard paprika)
- 2 tablespoons drained capers
- Finely chopped fresh parsley or basil, for garnish
- Fresh ground black pepper

Preparation

1. Preheat the oven to 425 degrees Fahrenheit.
2. Chop the tomatoes, shallot, garlic, and lemon as noted above.
3. Place the chopped vegetables and lemon slices in the bottom of a 9 x 13" baking dish and mix with 1 tablespoon olive oil, ¼ teaspoon salt, and fresh ground black pepper. Crumble the feta cheese into rough chunks and add it to the pan, tossing gently to combine.
4. Pat the tilapia dry. Rub it with 1 tablespoon olive oil and ½ teaspoon kosher salt, split between the filets. Place it on top of the vegetables and feta in the pan. Sprinkle both fillets with the Italian seasoning and a few grinds fresh ground black pepper, then add the red pepper flakes and smoked paprika. Sprinkle the capers over the top.
5. Place the pan in the oven and bake for 20 to 25 minutes (depending on the thickness of the fish), until the fish is flaky and the internal temperature is 140 degrees Fahrenheit when measured with a food thermometer. Garnish with chopped parsley and remove the lemon slices when serving (or eat them if you like!).

Nutrition fact

Total Fat 16.2g Saturated Fat 6.3g 2%Total Carbohydrate 6.3g 4%Dietary Fiber 1.2g Sugars 3.7g 78%Protein 39.2g 7%Vitamin A 67.1µg 18%Vitamin C 15.9mg 13%Calcium 171.9mg 8%Iron 1.5mg 54%Vitamin D 10.8µg 15%Magnesium 62.7mg 16%Potassium 739mg 29%Vitamin B6 0.5mg 132%Vitamin B12 3.2µg

Mediterranean Tuna Salad

Prep Time: 10 minutes
Cook Time: 0 minutes
Servings 2

Ingredients

- 1 red bell pepper, finely diced
- 1 small shallot, minced
- 1 cup chopped English cucumber (or standard cucumber, peeled)
- 2 5-ounce cans white meat tuna
- 3 tablespoons capers, drained
- 2 tablespoon white wine vinegar
- 1 tablespoon olive oil
- 1 tablespoon Dijon mustard
- ¼ teaspoon kosher salt
- 2 tablespoons feta cheese crumbles (optional)

Preparation

1. Prep the red pepper, shallot and English cucumber as noted above.
2. Drain the tuna and place it in a medium bowl: mash it lightly with a fork. Add the chopped vegetables, capers, white wine vinegar, olive oil, Dijon mustard, feta (if using) and kosher salt and stir to combine. Taste and add more salt if desired. Stores up to 3 days refrigerated.

Nutrition fact

Total Fat 11.6g Saturated Fat 2.2g 3%Total Carbohydrate 7.9g 9%Dietary Fiber 2.4g Sugars 4.4g 70%Protein 35g 14%Vitamin A 129µg 108%Vitamin C 97.6mg 3%Calcium 41.3mg 12%Iron 2.2mg 28%Vitamin D 5.7µg 16%Magnesium 68.4mg 13%Potassium 597.1mg 33%Vitamin B6 0.6mg 69%Vitamin B12 1.7µg

Moroccan Chickpea Stew

Prep Time: 15 minutes
Cook Time: 30 minutes
Servings 6

Ingredients

- 2 cups dry quinoa or 1 recipe Easy Couscous*
- 1 large onion
- 3 cloves garlic
- 2 large sweet potatoes (about 1 ¾ pounds)
- 2 tablespoons olive oil
- 1 teaspoon each paprika and ground cumin
- ½ teaspoon each ground coriander, ground turmeric, and ground ginger
- ¼ teaspoon ground cinnamon
- ½ teaspoon each kosher salt and ground black pepper
- 2 pinches cayenne pepper 1 15-ounce can diced tomatoes
- 2 cups vegetable broth
- 15 ounce can chickpeas, drained (or 1 ½ cups cooked)
- 3 cups baby spinach (or chopped spinach)
- 2 tablespoons chopped fresh cilantro, for garnish
- 1 lemon, for garnish
- 1 cup Greek yogurt, for garnish

Preparation

1. Make the quinoa using the stovetop method or Instant Pot method. When it's done, sprinkle with a little kosher salt to taste.
2. Dice the onion and mince the garlic. Chop the sweet potatoes into bite-sized pieces.
3. In a large pot, heat the olive oil. Sauté the onion for about 5 minutes. Add the minced garlic and sauté about 1 minute.
4. Stir in the paprika, cumin, coriander, turmeric, ginger, cinnamon, kosher salt, black pepper, andcayenne pepper. Stir about 30 seconds, then add diced tomatoes and broth.
5. Bring to a boil, then add sweet potatoes and drained and rinsed chickpeas. Simmer 25 to 30 minutes until the potatoes are tender. Stir in the spinach in the last 2 minutes.
6. Serve over the quinoa, garnished with chopped cilantro, fresh squeezed lemon juice, and a dollop of Greek yogurt.

Nutrition fact

Total Fat 9.6g Saturated Fat 1.3g 22%Total Carbohydrate 59.9g 34%Dietary Fiber 9.4g Sugars 4.6g 26%Protein 12.9g 45%Vitamin A 407.3µg 14%Vitamin C 12.7mg 7%Calcium 94.4mg 26%Iron 4.7mg 0%Vitamin D 0µg 38%Magnesium 160.2mg 17%Potassium 795.3mg 45%Vitamin B6 0.8mg 0%Vitamin B12 0µg

Lemon Dill Salmon

Prep Time: 10 minutes
Cook Time: 10 minutes
Servings 4

Ingredients

For the lemon dill sauce (makes about ¾ cup)

- 2 tablespoons finely chopped dill
- ¼ cup Greek yogurt
- 6 tablespoons mayonnaise
- 1 tablespoon lemon juice
- ¼ teaspoon garlic powder
- ¼ teaspoon onion powder
- ⅛ teaspoon kosher salt
- 2 teaspoons water

For the salmon

- 4 salmon fillets (skin on or off)
- Kosher salt
- Black pepper

Preparation

1. Preheat the oven to 450 degrees Fahrenheit.*
2. Generously sprinkle the salmon with kosher salt and fresh ground black pepper. Place it on a parchment-lined baking sheet.
3. Bake the salmon for about 10 minutes until flaky and just cooked; test it with a fork to assess doneness. Watch the salmon to make sure not to overcook; the timing can vary based on the thickness of the salmon and variations between ovens.
4. While the salmon bakes, mix together the sauce Ingredients, adding the water last. Use the water to bring it to a loose, drizzle-able consistency. (You may need a touch more depending on your yogurt brand.)
5. Serve the salmon and garnish each fillet with 2 tablespoons of the lemon dill sauce. Save leftover sauce refrigerated.

Nutrition fact

Total Fat 21.8g Saturated Fat 3.8g 1%Total Carbohydrate 2.2g 1%Dietary Fiber 0.3g Sugars 0.9g 55%Protein 27.4g 7%Vitamin A 63.7µg 3%Vitamin C 2.3mg 4%Calcium 58.2mg 7%Iron 1.3mg 161%Vitamin D 32.1µg 10%Magnesium 43.7mg 11%Potassium 503.6mg 51%Vitamin B6 0.9mg 229%Vitamin B12 5.5µg

Quick Hummus Bowls

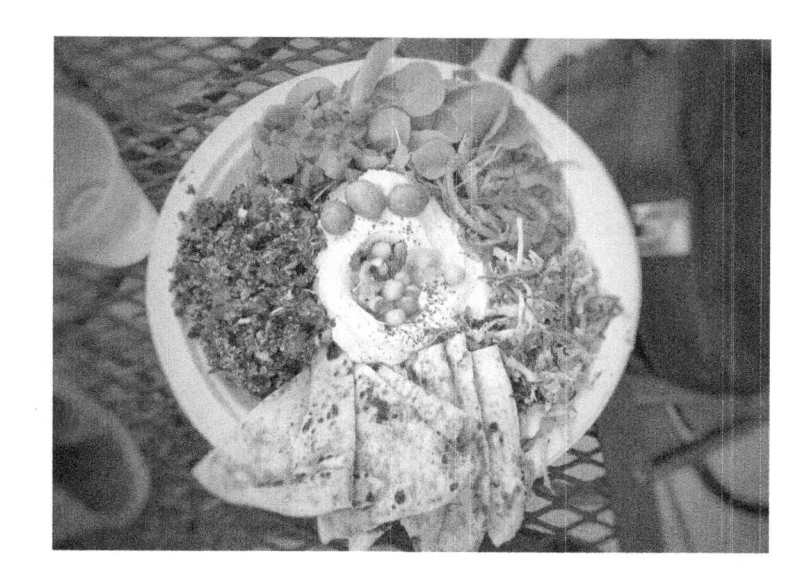

Prep Time: 10 minutes
Cook Time: 0 minutes
Servings 1

Ingredients

- ⅓ cup hummus
- 8 English cucumber slices (or standard cucumber, peeled)
- 1 handful red onion slices (or shallot)
- 1 handful cherry tomatoes, sliced
- 1 handful Kalamata olives
- 2 tablespoons feta cheese, to sprinkle (optional or use vegan feta for vegan)
- 1 handful baby greens or chopped lettuce (optional)
- ½ cup cooked rice or packaged pre-cooked rice (optional) or Easy Couscous or Easy Orzo
- 1 pita bread, pita chips, or gluten free crackers
- Optional toppings: Jarred Calabrian chilis or roasted red peppers, caper berries, fresh herbs, frozen or homemade falafel, etc.

Preparation

1. Place greens and rice in the bowl, if using (try packaged pre-cooked rice for a quick shortcut). If using rice, season it with salt and a drizzle of olive oil.
2. Top with hummus, sliced cucumber, sliced red onions, sliced tomatoes, olives and feta cheese. Eat with pita wedges, using the hummus as a dip / dressing for the veggies.

Nutrition fact

Total Fat 17.1g Saturated Fat 4.5g 31%Total Carbohydrate 86.2g 36%Dietary Fiber 10.1g Sugars 4.9g 34%Protein 17g23%Vitamin A 203.8µg 28%Vitamin C 25.5mg 17%Calcium 219.1mg 33%Iron 5.9mg 1%Vitamin D 0.2µg 28%Magnesium 117.1mg 14%Potassium 636.4mg 44%Vitamin B6 0.7mg 13%Vitamin B12 0.3µg

Quinoa Stuffed Peppers Recipe

Prep Time: 10 minutes
Cook Time: 35 minutes
Servings 6

Ingredients

- 6 multi-colored bell peppers
- 1 cup simplynature Organic Quinoa
- 4 garlic cloves
- 3 medium shallots (1 cup chopped)
- ¼ cup plus 1 tablespoon chopped parsley
- ¾ cup chopped Southern Grove Shelled Pistachios
- 2 tablespoons simplynature Organic Extra Virgin Olive Oil
- ¼ teaspoon red pepper flakes
- 1 teaspoon paprika
- 1 teaspoon dried oregano
- 2 tablespoons lemon juice plus zest from ½ lemon
- ½ teaspoon sea salt
- ¼ teaspoon black pepper
- ¼ cup feta cheese crumbles (optional)

Preparation

1. Preheat oven to 425°F.
2. Wash the peppers and cut them in half lengthwise; remove the stems and seeds. Line a baking sheet with parchment paper, then place the peppers on top. Bake with the cut side down for 15 minutes, then remove from the oven, flip to cut side up, and sprinkle with a pinch of salt and pepper. Bake another 15 minutes until tender.
3. Meanwhile, cook the quinoa (or use our Instant Pot quinoa method): Rinse the quinoa and drain it completely, then place it in a saucepan with 2 cups water. Bring to a boil, then reduce the heat to low, cover, and simmer where the water is just bubbling for 17 to 20 minutes until the water has been completely absorbed. (Check by pulling back the quinoa with a fork to see if water remains.) Turn off the heat and let sit with the lid on to steam for at least 5 minutes.
4. Mince the garlic, shallot and parsley. Chop the pistachios. In a large skillet, heat 2 tablespoons olive oil. Add the garlic, shallot and red pepper flakes and sauté 1 to 2 minutes until the shallot is translucent and the garlic is fragrant. Remove from the heat, then stir in the cooked quinoa, pistachios, ¼ cup parsley, paprika, oregano, lemon juice and zest, sea salt and black pepper. Taste and add another few pinches of salt to taste. Spoon the filling into the roasted pepper halves. Garnish with a small sprinkling of remaining parsley and feta cheese crumbles. Serve any additional filling on the side.

Nutrition fact

Total Fat 13.9g Saturated Fat 1.8g 12%Total Carbohydrate 32.5g 25%Dietary Fiber 6.9g Sugars 6.9g 18%Protein 8.9g 23%Vitamin A 203.4µg 175%Vitamin C 157.1mg 5%Calcium 61.3mg 16%Iron 2.9mg 0%Vitamin D 0µg 23%Magnesium 96.4mg 14%Potassium 641.3mg 48%Vitamin B6 0.8mg 0%Vitamin B12 0µg

Spanish Paella Recipe

Prep Time: 15 minutes
Cook Time: 30 minutes
Servings 4

Ingredients

- 1 medium yellow onion
- 6 garlic cloves
- 2 to 3 roma or plum tomatoes (1 ½ cups finely chopped)
- ¼ cup olive oil, divided
- 1/2 pound shrimp, peel and deveined*
- 1 ½ teaspoons smoked paprika, divided
- ¼ teaspoon red pepper flakes
- 1 large pinch saffron
- 1 ½ teaspoons kosher salt, divided
- 3 cups seafood stock or vegetable stock
- 1 ½ cups short grain Bomba rice or arborio rice
- ¼ cup frozen peas, thawed under water
- ½ cup artichoke hearts, quartered
- 1 to 2 roasted red bell peppers, cut into strips
- Lemon wedges from ½ lemon
- Chopped parsley, for garnish

Preparation

1. Prep the vegetables: Mince the onion. Mince the garlic. Finely chop the tomatoes, removing the cores but keeping the seeds with their juices.
2. Measure out the Ingredients: Measure out all the remaining Ingredients before you start. The cooking process goes fast!
3. Cook the shrimp: Dry the shrimp and add it to a bowl with ½ teaspoon smoked paprika and ¼ teaspoon kosher salt. In your largest skillet or a 4-serving paella pan, heat 1 tablespoon olive oil over medium heat. Add the shrimp and saute until it is just barely opaque, about 1 to 2 minutes per side. Remove the shrimp and set it aside.
4. Cook the paella: In the same pan, heat 3 tablespoons olive oil on medium heat. Saute the onion and garlic until just translucent, about 3 minutes, stirring frequently. Add the chopped tomatoes, the remaining 1 teaspoon smoked paprika and red pepper flakes, and cook until the tomatoes have broken down and most of the liquid is evaporated, about 5 minutes. Stir in the stock, saffron and 1 ¼ teaspoon kosher salt. Sprinkle the rice evenly across the broth and tap the pan with a spoon to evenly spread the rice. Bring to a medium simmer and cook without stirring until liquid is absorbed, about 18 to 22 minutes (adjust the cook time as necessary if using a skillet).
5. Adjust the heat as necessary: If your pan is large enough to span multiple burners on your stovetop, adjust the heat on each burner so you achieve a steady medium simmer. Rotate the pan every few minutes for an even cook.
6. Add the artichoke, peas and roasted red pepper: When the top of the rice is beginning to show through the liquid (about 10 minutes into the cook time), press the artichokes and peas lightly into the rice. Add the strips of red pepper over the top.
7. Assess whether the paella is done: In last few minutes, carefully watch the paella and rotate pan more frequently. As the paella finishes, you'll see the steam start to slow down as the water cooks out. If desired, peek at the bottom of a pan by using a knife to scrape back the rice — you shouldn't see any standing water. The sound will start to change from a simmer to a crackle. This indicates

the crust is forming. Let the crackling continue for about 2 minutes before removing from the heat. If you smell any burning, remove immediately.
8. Add the shrimp and serve: When the paella is done, add the shrimp to top of paella and squeeze the lemon wedges onto the top of the pan. Sprinkle with a pinch or two of kosher salt and add the parsley, if using. Serve with additional lemon wedges.

Nutrition fact

Total Fat 14.6g Saturated Fat 2.1g 24%Total Carbohydrate 65.4g 10%Dietary Fiber 2.9g Sugars 5.3g 36%Protein 17.9g 4%Vitamin A 40.1μg 17%Vitamin C 15.3mg 4%Calcium 56.3mg 4%Iron 0.8mg 0%Vitamin D 0μg 10%Magnesium 41.8mg 10%Potassium 483.9mg 7%Vitamin B6 0.1mg 0%Vitamin B12 0μg

Tuscan Soup with White Beans

Prep Time: 10 minutes
Cook Time: 20 minutes
Servings 6

Ingredients

- 1 bulb fennel
- 2 bunches Tuscan kale or other dark leafy greens (Swiss chard, spinach, mustard greens)
- 2 15-ounce cans cannellini beans
- 2 tablespoons olive oil
- 2 28-ounce cans diced tomatoes (San Marzano, if possible)
- 4 cups vegetable broth (or canned broth)
- 2 cups water
- ½ teaspoon red pepper flakes
- 1 teaspoon dried basil
- ½ teaspoon smoked paprika
- 1 teaspoon kosher salt
- Pecorino cheese to garnish (optional)

Preparation

1. Chop the fennel bulb (reserve some sprigs for a garnish). Wash and roughly chop the kale. Drain and rinse the cannellini beans.
2. In a large pot or Dutch oven, heat the olive oil over medium high heat, then sauté the fennel for 5 minutes.
3. Add the canned tomatoes with their juices and simmer for 8 minutes.
4. Add the vegetable broth, water and cannellini beans. Bring to a boil.
5. Reduce to a simmer and add the red pepper flakes, dried basil, smoked paprika, and kosher salt.
6. Add the kale and simmer until tender, about 5 minutes. Serve garnished with grated Pecorino cheese and fennel sprigs. Store refrigerated for 3 days or frozen up to 3 months.

Nutrition fact

Total Fat 5.5g Saturated Fat 0.9g 14%Total Carbohydrate 38.4g 34%Dietary Fiber 9.4g Sugars 6.7g 23%Protein 11.6g 15%Vitamin A 130.5µg 38%Vitamin C 34.1mg 11%Calcium 146.2mg 26%Iron 4.7mg 0%Vitamin D 0µg 22%Magnesium 93.1mg 23%Potassium 1100.7mg 15%Vitamin B6 0.2mg 0%Vitamin B12 0µg

Mediterranean Couscous Bowls Recipe

Prep Time: 20 minutes
Cook Time: 5 minutes
Servings 4

Ingredients

For the chickpeas (or substitute Seasoned Lentils)

- 1 ½ cups cooked or 1 15-ounce can chickpeas (try Instant Pot Chickpeas)
- 1 tablespoon olive oil
- ½ teaspoon cumin
- ½ teaspoon kosher salt

For the couscous

- 1 cup whole wheat couscous (substitute cooked quinoa for gluten-free)
- ¾ teaspoon kosher salt
- 1 tablespoon olive oil
- 2 tablespoons finely chopped parsley

For the bowl

- 1 small cucumber
- 1 pint cherry tomatoes
- 8 cups salad greens
- 1 recipe Best Tahini Sauce
-

Preparation

1. Make the chickpeas: If using dry chickpeas, cook them using our Instant Pot chickpeas method (in under 1 hour!) Or our Dutch oven method. If using canned, drain and rinse them. In a medium bowl, stir them together with the olive oil, cumin, and kosher salt.
2. Make the couscous: In a medium pot, bring 1 ¼ cups water to a boil. Add couscous and ½ teaspoon kosher salt. Bring to a boil, then remove from the heat, cover, and let stand for 5 minutes. When done, stir in the olive oil, another ¼ teaspoon kosher salt, and the parsley.
3. Make the dressing: Go to Best Tahini Sauce.
4. Assemble the bowls: Peel and chop the cucumber. Slice the tomatoes in half. In a large shallow bowl, place the greens, then top with couscous, chickpeas, cucumber, and tomatoes. Drizzle with tahini dressing (about 2 tablespoons per bowl). Serve immediately. Leftovers stay in the refrigerator for a few days: keep all components separate for maximum freshness.

Nutrition fact

Total Fat 23.5g Saturated Fat 3.3g 20%Total Carbohydrate 56.1g 31%Dietary Fiber 8.8g Sugars 2.3g 31%Protein 15.6g 32%Vitamin A 285.1µg 30%Vitamin C 27.4mg 11%Calcium 149.2mg 25%Iron 4.5mg 0%Vitamin D 0µg 28%Magnesium 119mg 15%Potassium 717mg 38%Vitamin B6 0.6mg 0%Vitamin B12

Greek Nachos with Cilantro Sauce

Prep Time: 25 minutes
Cook Time: 0 minutes
Servings   4

Ingredients

- 1 recipe Homemade Pita Chips (with za'atar seasoning optional)
- 1/2 English cucumber
- 1 cup quartered grape tomatoes
- ½ cup diced Kalamata olives
- 15-ounce can navy beans
- 1 tablespoon olive oil
- ¼ teaspoon kosher salt, plus more for sprinkling
- Black pepper
- Creamy Cilantro Sauce, to serve

Preparation

1. Start soaking the cashews for the Creamy Cilantro Sauce (or soak the cashews in advance or overnight).
2. Make the homemade pita chips.
3. Dice the cucumber and quarter the tomatoes; sprinkle both lightly with kosher salt. Chop the olives. Drain and rinse the beans; in a small bowl, mix the beans with the olive oil, kosher salt, and a few grinds of fresh ground black pepper.
4. Make the Creamy Cilantro Sauce.
5. To serve, place the pita chips on a plate. Top with veggies and beans, and drizzle with cilantro sauce and additional olive oil (if desired). Sprinkle with torn cilantro and serve.

Best Healthy Pizza

Prep Time: 60 minutes
Cook Time: 7 minutes
Servings 8

Ingredients

- 1 ball Easy Thin Crust Dough
- ½ cup Easy Pizza Sauce
- 1/2 yellow bell pepper
- 1/2 red bell pepper
- 1/4 medium red onion
- 1 garlic clove
- ½ teaspoon dried oregano, plus more for garnish
- 1 tablespoon olive oil
- ½ tablespoon capers, drained
- ¼ cup grated Parmesan cheese
- ½ cup baby arugula
- Kosher salt
- Olive oil
- Semolina flour or cornmeal, for dusting the pizza peel

Preparation

1. Make the pizza dough: Follow the Easy Thin Crust Pizza Dough recipe to prepare the dough. (This takes about 15 minutes to make and 45 minutes to rest.)
2. Place a pizza stone in the oven and preheat to 500°F. OR preheat your pizza oven (here's the pizza oven we use).
3. Make the pizza sauce: Make the Easy Pizza Sauce.
4. Prepare the toppings: Thinly slice the peppers. Thinly slice the red onion. Thinly slice the garlic. In a skillet, add 1 tablespoon olive oil and ¼ teaspoon kosher salt. Saute the vegetables, stirring often, for about 7 to 10 minutes, until browned and very soft. Stir in the oregano and remove from the heat.
5. Bake the pizza: When the oven is ready, dust a pizza peel with cornmeal or semolina flour. (If you don't have a pizza peel, you can use a rimless baking sheet or the back of a rimmed baking sheet. But a pizza peel is well worth the investment!) Stretch the dough into a circle; see How to Stretch Pizza Dough for instructions. Then gently place the dough onto the pizza peel.
6. Spread the pizza sauce over the dough using the back of a spoon to create a thin layer. Sprinkle with the vegetables, drained capers, and Parmesan cheese.
7. Use the pizza peel to carefully transfer the pizza onto the preheated pizza stone. Bake the pizza until the cheese and crust are nicely browned, about 5 to 7 minutes in the oven (or 1 minute in a pizza oven).
8. While the pizza is baking, mix the baby arugula with a drizzle of olive oil and a pinch of kosher salt. When the pizza is done, top with the arugula. Slice into pieces and serve immediately.

Nutrition fact

Total Fat 3.2g Saturated Fat 0.8g 5%Total Carbohydrate 13.7g 3%Dietary Fiber 0.8g Sugars 0.9g 6%Protein 2.9g 1%Vitamin A 13µg 9%Vitamin C 7.7mg 3%Calcium 42.5mg 5%Iron 0.9mg 0%Vitamin D 0µg 2%Magnesium 8.6mg 2%Potassium 84.7mg 3%Vitamin B6 0mg 2%Vitamin B12 0µg

Simple Red Lentil Soup

Prep Time: 10 minutes
Cook Time: 15 minutes
Servings 6

Ingredients

- 3 large carrots
- 1 medium yellow onion
- 3 celery ribs
- 6 garlic cloves
- ¼ cup olive oil
- 2 quarts vegetable broth
- 1 cup water
- 1 pound split red lentils*
- 1 ½ tablespoons smoked paprika
- 1 ½ teaspoons lemon zest
- 1 teaspoon kosher salt
- Fresh ground black pepper
- Greek yogurt or sour cream (or cashew cream for vegan), for serving
- Cilantro, for serving

Preparation

1. Peel the carrots. Finely dice the carrot, onion, and celery. Mince the garlic.
2. In a large pot or Dutch oven, heat the olive oil over medium heat. Add the onion, carrots and celery, and sauté until the carrots are tender, about 5 to 7 minutes.
3. Stir in the garlic and sauté for 1 minute. Add the broth, water, red lentils, smoked paprika, lemon zest, kosher salt and fresh ground pepper.
4. Bring to a low simmer, then cover halfway and gently simmer until the lentils are just soft but before they start to break apart, about 7 to 10 minutes. Watch closely and taste to assess doneness. The finished soup should be brothy with the lentils just soft; cooking past this point yields a very thick stew which is just as delicious but less soup-like. (If you'd like, you can add handfuls of greens in the last few minutes, like chopped spinach or kale).
5. Taste and add additional salt to taste, and a few grinds black pepper. Leftovers can become very thick, so you can add a little water or broth when reheating.

Nutrition fact

Total Fat 13.8gsaturated Fat 2.8g23%Total Carbohydrate 62.6g 40%Dietary Fiber 11.2g Sugars 8g 48%Protein 23.8g 41%Vitamin A 366.5µg 10%Vitamin C 8.6mg 10%Calcium 134.8mg 35%Iron 6.3mg 0%Vitamin D 0µg 16%Magnesium 67.2mg 19%Potassium 916.4mg 31%Vitamin B6 0.5mg 15%Vitamin B12 0.4µg

Vegetarian Tortellini Soup

Prep Time: 5 minutes
Cook Time: 30 minutes
Servings 3-4

Ingredients

- 2 tablespoons olive oil
- 1 onion
- 2 garlic cloves
- 2 tablespoons tomato paste
- 1 teaspoon paprika
- 2 carrots
- 2 celery stalks
- 14-ounce can crushed fire roasted tomatoes
- 1 quart vegetable broth
- ½ teaspoon kosher salt
- Freshly ground black pepper
- 9 ounces good-quality fresh tortellini (aka tortelloni, found in the refrigerated section)
- 1 handful basil leaves
- Grated Parmesan cheese, for garnish

Preparation

1. Mince the garlic. Dice the onion. Peel the carrot; chop the carrot and celery into bite-sized pieces.
2. Heat the olive oil in a large saucepan or Dutch oven and saute the onion and garlic with the tomato paste and paprika over medium-low heat for 5 minutes, or until the onion begins to soften.
3. Add the carrots and celery and saute for another 5 minutes, or until the onion has softened.
4. Add the tomatoes and vegetable broth to the pan with the kosher salt and several grinds of black pepper and bring to a boil. Reduce the heat and simmer with the lid ajar for 15 minutes, or until the vegetables are cooked.
5. Add the tortellini to the pan and cook according to the package instructions, before stirring in the basil leaves.
6. Serve hot topped with a sprinkling of Parmesan cheese and a drizzle of oil. (We had fresh thyme on hand, so we garnished with that as well!)

Nutrition fact

Total Fat 12.1g Saturated Fat 3.4g 17%Total Carbohydrate 45.6g 19%Dietary Fiber 5.2g Sugars 8.4g 22%Protein 10.9g 65%Vitamin A 583.1µg 20%Vitamin C 18.4mg 12%Calcium 156.2mg 12%Iron 2.2mg 0%Vitamin D 0µg 10%Magnesium 40.4mg 12%Potassium 555mg 17%Vitamin B6 0.3mg 4%Vitamin B12 0.1µg

Easy Shakshuka with Feta

Prep Time: 10 minutes
Cook Time: 25 minutes
Servings 4

Ingredients

- 1 teaspoon coriander seeds*
- 1 teaspoon cumin seeds*
- 1 teaspoon fennel seeds*
- 2 tablespoons olive oil
- 1 red bell pepper
- 1 large yellow onion
- 1 teaspoon smoked paprika
- 1 teaspoon kosher salt, plus more for sprinkling
- 1 28 ounce can diced tomatoes
- 1 15 ounce can white beans, drained and rinsed
- 4 to 6 large eggs, to your preference
- Freshly ground black pepper
- ½ cup fresh parsley or cilantro leaves
- ½ cup feta cheese crumbles

Preparation

1. Thinly slice the pepper. Thinly slice the onion.
2. Set a dry skillet, preferably cast iron, over medium heat. Add the coriander, cumin, and fennel seeds, then toast until fragrant, about 2 minutes. Carefully transfer the seeds to a plate to cool, then grind in a mortar and pestle or spice grinder.
3. Heat the olive oil in the same skillet over medium-high heat. Add the bell pepper and onion in an even layer, then do not be tempted to stir or fuss with them. Let them get a good, dark char, 3 to 4 minutes, before giving a quick stir and cooking a bit more until nearly all of the pepper and onion are blackened in parts. This process will take about 10 minutes.
4. Add the ground spices, paprika, and kosher salt. Stir for 1 minute before carefully tipping in the tomatoes. Let this mixture come to a simmer before stirring in the white beans. Bring everything to a gently boil, then lower the heat to a steady simmer. Simmer for 5 minutes, or until the tomatoes have thickened.
5. Carve out a little divot for each of the eggs you plan to cook, then carefully crack them in. Add a bit of kosher salt and black pepper to each egg then cover the skillet with a lid (or sheet pan if you can't find a matching lid). Cook over low heat until the eggs are just set, 4 to 6 minutes.
6. Chop the cilantro. Finish by garnishing with the fresh herbs and feta. Serve immediately.

Nutrition fact

Total Fat 19g Saturated Fat 5.7g 7%Total Carbohydrate 18.1g 16%Dietary Fiber 4.6g Sugars 5.3g 27%Protein 13.3g 19%Vitamin A 168.5µg 60%Vitamin C 54mg 14%Calcium 182.2mg 19%Iron 3.5mg 11%Vitamin D 2.2µg 14%Magnesium 58.5mg 7%Potassium 344.8mg 20%Vitamin B6 0.3mg 32%Vitamin B12 0.8µg

Shrimp Marinara

Prep Time: 10 minutes
Cook Time: 20 minutes
Servings 4

Ingredients

For the marinara sauce

- 28 ounce can crushed fire roasted tomatoes (or best quality crushed tomatoes)*
- 2 tablespoons olive oil
- 1 tablespoon balsamic vinegar
- 2 teaspoons garlic powder
- 1 teaspoon dried oregano
- 1 teaspoon kosher salt
- 8 fresh basil leaves, plus more for the garnish

For the shrimp and pasta

- 8 ounces spaghetti noodles
- 1 pound large shrimp, deveined (peeled or unpeeled)
- 2 teaspoons dried basil
- ¼ teaspoon kosher salt
- 2 tablespoons butter (or olive oil)
- Parmesan cheese, for garnish (optional)
-

Preparation

1. Thaw the shrimp (according to the package instructions, or see the section above). When thawed, pat the shrimp dry with a paper towel or clean rag.
2. Bring a large pot of salted water to a boil. Boil the pasta until it is al dente (start tasting a few minutes before the package recommends: you want it to be tender but still a little firm on the inside). Then drain.
3. In a large skillet, heat the butter on medium high heat. Add the shrimp, basil and kosher salt. Cook the shrimp for 1 to 2 minutes per side until almost cooked through, turning them with tongs (they will cook additionally when you add the marinara at the end). Remove the shrimp from the pan into a bowl, leaving the juices inside the skillet.
4. In same skillet, add the marinara sauce Ingredients, scraping any bits off of the bottom of skillet as you stir it together. Bring to a simmer, then cover and cook for 15 minutes.
5. Add shrimp to the skillet and remove the heat. Serve over pasta and topped with Parmesan cheese (optional) and chopped basil.

Nutrition fact

Total Fat 14.3g Saturated Fat 4.9g 17%Total Carbohydrate 45.8g 9%Dietary Fiber 2.5g Sugars 3.1g 62%Protein 30.9g 7%Vitamin A 65.1µg 6%Vitamin C 5.2mg 7%Calcium 97.1mg 15%Iron 2.8mg 0%Vitamin D 0µg 18%Magnesium 76.5mg 12%Potassium 542.6mg 8%Vitamin B6 0.1mg1%Vitamin B12 0µg

Simple Chickpea Salad

Prep Time: 5 minutes
Cook Time: 0 minutes
Servings 2

Ingredients

- 15-ounce can chickpeas (or 1 ½ cups cooked)
- ¼ cup bell pepper, diced
- ¼ cup English cucumber, chopped
- ½ tablespoon olive oil
- ½ tablespoon red wine vinegar
- ½ teaspoon kosher salt
- ½ teaspoon smoked paprika
- Fresh ground pepper
- 1 pinch celery seed or fresh torn herbs (parsley, dill, basil, etc), optional

Preparation

1. Drain and rinse the chickpeas.
2. Dice the bell pepper. Chop the cucumber (peel it if you're using a standard cucumber; English cucumber doesn't need to be peeled).
3. In a bowl, mix together all Ingredients. Taste and add salt as desired.

Nutrition fact

Total Fat 7.1g Saturated Fat 0.9g 9%Total Carbohydrate 25.9g 30%Dietary Fiber 8.4g Sugars 1g 18%Protein 9.1g 4%Vitamin A 31.7µg 27%Vitamin C 24.3mg 5%Calcium 66.4mg 13%Iron 2.3mg 0%Vitamin D 0µg 13%Magnesium 52.5mg 7%Potassium 317.6mg 54%Vitamin B6 0.9mg 0%Vitamin B12 0µg

Quinoa Tabbouleh

Prep Time: 10 minutes
Cook Time: 20 minutes
Servings 8

Ingredients

- 1 cup dry quinoa
- 2 cups finely chopped curly parsley (2 bunches)
- ¼ cup chopped fresh mint
- 3 green onions
- 2 medium tomatoes, seeded and finely chopped (1 cup)
- 1/2 English cucumber (1 cup finely chopped)
- 6 tablespoons lemon juice
- ¼ cup olive oil
- ½ teaspoon kosher salt
- Fresh ground black pepper

Preparation

1. Make the quinoa: Rinse the quinoa using a fine mesh strainer, then drain it completely. Place it in a saucepan with 2 cups water and ¼ teaspoon kosher salt. Bring to a boil, then reduce the heat to low. Cover the pot and simmer where the water is just bubbling for about 17 to 20 minutes, until the water has been completely absorbed. (Check by pulling back the quinoa with a fork to see if water remains.) Turn off the heat and let sit with the lid on to steam for 5 minutes, then fluff the quinoa with a fork.
2. Cool the quinoa to room temperature: To do this quickly, dump the quinoa onto a baking sheet and spread it in an even layer. Pop it in the freezer for 2 to 3 minutes until cooled to room temperature. Or, you can make the quinoa in advance and let it sit at room temp or refrigerate until serving (it cools fastest spread on a baking sheet).
3. Meanwhile, chop the vegetables: Finely chop the parsley and mint. Thinly slice the green onions. Finely chop the tomato, removing the core and seeds. Finely chop the cucumber (if you're using a standard cucumber and not English cucumber, remove the seeds too.)
4. Add the dressing: Juice the lemon and whisk it together with the olive oil. In a large bowl, toss the quinoa and vegetables with the dressing, kosher salt and pepper. Taste and adjust flavors as necessary. Serve immediately or refrigerate for 3 to 4 days.

Nutrition fact

Total Fat 8.5g Saturated Fat 1.2g 6%Total Carbohydrate 16.2g 8%Dietary Fiber 2.3g Sugars 0.8g 7%Protein 3.6g 8%Vitamin A 71.5µg 29%Vitamin C 25.9mg 3%Calcium 35.6mg 11%Iron 2mg 0%Vitamin D 0µg 13%Magnesium 52.6mg 5%Potassium 249.9mg 8%Vitamin B6 0.1mg 0%Vitamin B12 0µg

Baked Shrimp with Feta and Tomatoes

Prep Time: 10 minutes
Cook Time: 20 minutes
Servings 4

Ingredients

- 1 medium yellow onion
- 2 cloves garlic
- 1 tablespoon olive oil
- 28-ounce can diced fire roasted tomatoes
- ¼ cup fresh parsley, minced
- 1 pound medium raw shrimp, peeled, deveined and shells removed (thawed if frozen)
- 2/3 cup feta crumbled cheese
- ½ teaspoon kosher salt
- Fresh ground pepper
- Lemon

Preparation

1. Preheat oven to 425°F.
2. Finely dice the onion. Mince the garlic.
3. In a large ovenproof skillet over medium-high heat, heat the olive oil. Add the onion and cook until soft, 3-5 minutes. Add the garlic and cook until fragrant, about 30 seconds more. Add the tomatoes and bring to a simmer. Reduce the heat and let the sauce simmer for 5 to 8 minutes, until the juices thicken a bit.
4. While the vegetables cook, mince ¼ cup fresh parsley.
5. Remove the sauce from the heat, and stir in the parsley, shrimp, feta cheese, kosher salt, and several grinds of fresh pepper.
6. Place the skillet in the oven and bake until the shrimp are cooked through, about 8-10 minutes. Garnish with fresh parsley and a squeeze of lemon juice. Serve immediately with bread, rice, quinoa, or couscous.

Easy Grilled Tilapia

Prep Time: 15 minutes
Cook Time: 8 minutes
Servings 4

Ingredients

- 4 4-ounce tilapia fillets, (wild caught if possible)
- 1 tablespoon olive oil
- 1 teaspoon kosher salt
- 2 teaspoons smoked paprika (also called pimentón)*
- ½ teaspoon garlic powder
- ½ teaspoon onion powder
- ⅛ teaspoon celery seed
- For serving: blistered tomatoes or chopped cherry tomatoes

Preparation

1. Preheat a grill to medium-high heat (375 to 450 degrees Fahrenheit).
2. Bring the tilapia to room temperature for about 15 minutes.
3. Pat the tilapia dry with a clean towel. Rub it with the olive oil and sprinkle it with the kosher salt and fresh ground pepper. Mix the smoked paprika, garlic powder, onion powder, and celery seed in a small bowl, then pat it on to the fish.
4. Grill the tilapia over indirect heat for 3 to 4 minutes, until it releases from the grates. Flip and cook another 3 to 4 minutes, until the fish is tender and just cooked through (internal temperature is 130-140F). Allow to rest for a few minutes, then serve, topping with blistered tomatoes if desired

Greek Salad

Prep Time: 10 minutes
Cook Time: 0 minutes
Servings 4

Ingredients

- 4 large ripe tomatoes
- 1/2 large red onion
- 2 large cucumbers
- 1 cup Kalamata olives
- 4 ounces high quality feta cheese: crumbled, cut into squares, or in a block (Greek feta, if you can find it!)
- 2 tablespoons olive oil
- 1 tablespoon red wine vinegar
- 1 teaspoon dried oregano
- 2 tablespoons capers (optional)
- Kosher salt

Preparation

1. Chop the tomatoes into rough chunks; remove and discard the seeds. Place the tomatoes in a large bowl and add a few pinches of kosher salt.
2. Thinly slice the red onion. Peel alternating strips from the cucumbers, making a striped pattern with the peel (alternatively, remove the peel entirely). Cut the cucumbers in half and use a spoon to remove the seeds; then, cut them into ½-inch pieces.
3. In a large bowl, combine the tomatoes, red onion, and cucumbers with the Kalamata olives, feta cheese crumbles, olive oil, and red wine vinegar. If desired, add the dried oregano and capers. Gently mix to combine.
4. Serve immediately, or let sit at room temperature for several minutes to allow the flavors to meld.

Nutrition fact

Total Fat 14.7g Saturated Fat 5.2g 4%Total Carbohydrate 12g 12%Dietary Fiber 3.2g Sugars 7.6g 12%Protein 5.8g 13%Vitamin A 113.8µg 30%Vitamin C 26.7mg 13%Calcium 167.1mg 6%Iron 1mg 1%Vitamin D 0.2µg 7%Magnesium 31.1mg 10%Potassium 491.2mg 17%Vitamin B6 0.3mg 18%Vitamin B12 0.4µg

Cozy White Bean Soup

Prep Time: 10 minutes
Cook Time: 25 minutes
Servings 6

Ingredients

- 3 tablespoons olive oil
- 1 large sweet yellow onion, finely diced
- 2 medium carrots, peeled and finely diced
- 3 celery ribs, thinly sliced
- 6 cloves garlic, minced
- 1 pound yellow or Yukon Gold potatoes, small diced
- 3 15-ounce cans (4 ½ cups cooked) cannellini beans, drained and rinsed (or Great Northern, navy, butter or other white bean)
- 2 quarts vegetable broth
- 1 ½ teaspoons lemon zest
- 1 ½ teaspoons dried tarragon*
- ¾ teaspoon kosher salt, or more to taste
- Fresh ground black pepper
- 5 to 6 leaves Tuscan kale, chopped into small pieces

Preparation

1. Prep the fresh Ingredients (see above).
2. In a Dutch oven or large pot, heat the olive oil over medium heat. Add the onion, carrot, and celery and sauté for 5 minutes.
3. Add the minced garlic and cook until just browned, about 1 minute. Add the potato, drained and rinsed white beans, vegetable broth, lemon zest, dried tarragon, kosher salt and fresh ground black pepper. Bring to a simmer and simmer for 15 minutes, until the potatoes are tender.
4. Remove 3 cups of the hot soup (including broth and vegetables) and carefully blend it in a blender or immersion blender. Then pour it back into the pot to create a lightly creamy broth (you can skip this step if you prefer and it still tastes great!).
5. Stir in the chopped kale and cook until wilted, about 2 minutes more. Taste and add any additional salt, to taste (depending on your brand of vegetable broth). Eat immediately or save leftovers refrigerated for up to 3 days or frozen for up to 3 months.

Nutrition fact

Total Fat 9.2g Saturated Fat 1.3g 26%Total Carbohydrate 70.5g 48%Dietary Fiber 13.4g Sugars 6.3g 34%Protein 16.9g 22%Vitamin A 194.2μg 15%Vitamin C 13.9mg 15%Calcium 194.5mg 36%Iron 6.5mg 0%Vitamin D 0μg 27%Magnesium 112.8mg 32%Potassium 1486.4mg 17%Vitamin B6 0.3mg 0%Vitamin

Pasta e Ceci (Italian Chickpea Soup)

Prep Time: 5 minutes
Cook Time: 25 minutes
Servings 6

Ingredients

- 1 medium onion
- 4 garlic cloves
- 1 bunch Tuscan kale (also called Lacinato or dinosaur kale, or cavolo nero)
- 2 tablespoons olive oil
- 2 tablespoons tomato paste
- 1 quart vegetable broth
- 28-ounce can crushed fire roasted tomatoes
- ½ cup chopped basil leaves, plus additional for serving if desired
- 1 15-ounce can chickpeas, drained and rinsed (or 1 ½ cups cooked)
- ½ teaspoon each dried oregano and dried thyme
- 2 pinches red pepper flakes
- Parmesan rind or ¼ cup grated Parmesan cheese* (omit for vegan)
- 1 teaspoon kosher salt
- ¾ cup short pasta (gluten-free or legume pasta: we used rigatoni)
- For the garnish: Grated Parmesan or Pecorino Romano cheese

Preparation

1. Peel and small dice the onion. Mince the garlic. Chop the kale into bite-sized pieces.
2. In a large pot or Dutch oven, heat the olive oil over medium high heat. Add the onion and saute for 5 to 6 minutes until the onions are just translucent. Add the garlic and tomato paste and saute for 1 minute.
3. Add the vegetable broth, tomatoes and juices, chopped basil, drained and rinsed chickpeas, oregano, thyme, red pepper flakes, Parmesan rind (or grated Parmesan) and kosher salt. Bring it to a simmer, then cook 10 minutes on medium low.
4. Add the pasta and kale and cook until pasta is just al dente, about 8 to 10 minutes.
5. Taste and add fresh ground black pepper and more kosher salt to taste. Remove the Parmesan rind. If desired, garnish with torn basil leaves and Parmesan cheese shavings. The soup will continue to thicken as it cools.

Nutrition fact

Total Fat 8.9g Saturated Fat 1.3g 13%Total Carbohydrate 35.5g 21%Dietary Fiber 5.9g Sugars 8g 15%Protein 7.4g 6%Vitamin A 52.4µg 19%Vitamin C 16.8mg 6%Calcium 72.1mg 15%Iron 2.6mg 0%Vitamin D 0µg 12%Magnesium 49.1mg 11%Potassium 495.1mg 32%Vitamin B6 0.5mg 0%Vitamin

Lentil Salad with Feta

Prep Time: 5 minutes
Cook Time: 25 minutes
Servings 6

Ingredients

For the lentil salad

- 2 tablespoons red wine vinegar
- 2 tablespoons lemon juice + zest of 1 lemon
- 1 teaspoon Dijon mustard
- ½ teaspoon onion powder
- 1 teaspoon dried oregano
- 6 tablespoons olive oil
- 1 shallot
- 2 tablespoons chopped fresh mint or chives (optional)
- ½ teaspoon kosher salt + fresh ground pepper
- 1 red pepper
- 1 cup baby arugula, plus more to serve
- 1 cup feta cheese crumbles, plus more for garnish
- ½ cup pistachios, plus more for garnish
- 3 radishes, for garnish

For the lentils

- 1 pound black beluga lentils or French lentils
- 1 quart vegetable broth+ 2 cups water
- 1 teaspoon kosher salt
- 1 teaspoon dried thyme
- ½ teaspoon garlic powder

Preparation

1. **For the lentils:** In a large saucepan or deep skillet, simmer the lentils with the broth, water, kosher salt, thyme, and garlic powder for about 15 to 20 minutes until tender. Drain excess liquid.
2. **Make the dressing:** In a large bowl, whisk together the red wine vinegar, lemon juice, lemon zest, Dijon mustard, onion powder, and oregano. Whisk in the olive oil 1 tablespoon at a time until it's creamy and emulsified.
3. **Chop the veggies:** Thinly slice the shallot. Thinly slice the red pepper, then cut the slices in half to make pieces about 2-inches long. If using the herbs, chop them.
4. **Mix together the salad:** Place the lentils in the large bowl with the dressing. Add the shallot, pepper, herbs, baby arugula, feta cheese, and pistachios. Add the ½ teaspoon kosher salt and fresh ground pepper and mix to combine.
5. **Serve:** If desired, serve over arugula. Garnish with thinly sliced radish, with an additional sprinkle of feta and pistachios. Refrigerate any leftovers for up to 4 days (if you're planning to make for lunches, omit the pistachios). It saves well and leftovers taste even better!

Nutrition fact

Total Fat 15g Saturated Fat 3.9g 11%Total Carbohydrate 31.5g 20%Dietary Fiber 5.6g Sugars 2.2g 29%Protein 14.7g 3%Vitamin A 27.4µg 4%Vitamin C 3.5mg 8%Calcium 100.9mg 19%Iron 3.4mg 1%Vitamin D 0.1µg 8%Magnesium 34mg 8%Potassium 398mg 25%Vitamin B6 0.4mg 11%Vitamin

Pan Seared Scallops

Prep Time: 10 minutes
Cook Time: 5 minutes
Servings 4

Ingredients

- 1 pound sea scallops, thawed if frozen
- Kosher salt
- 2 tablespoons neutral oil
- 1 tablespoon salted butter
- Lemon wedges, for serving

Preparation

1. Thaw the scallops, if frozen (see above).
2. Brine the scallops: In a shallow dish, mix together 4 cups room temperature water and 2 tablespoons kosher salt. Place the scallops in the water and wait for 10 minutes.
3. Remove the scallops and dry thoroughly. Lightly season with a several pinches kosher salt.
4. Heat the oil in a large skillet over high heat. If using a medium skillet, cook the scallops in two batches. Once the oil is hot, add the scallops and cook without turning for 2 to 3 minutes, until an even brown crust clearly forms on bottom.
5. Flip scallops with tongs. Cook additional 2 to 3 minutes on the other side, until a crust just forms on bottom and the center of the scallop is almost opaque.
6. Turn off the heat and add the butter. When it melts, spoon the melted butter over the scallops and serve with a squeeze of lemon. Or, go to Lemon Herb Scallop Sauce to make a 2 minute pan sauce.

Nutrition fact

Total Fat 10.4g Saturated Fat 3g 1%Total Carbohydrate 3.6g 0%Dietary Fiber 0g Sugars 0g 27%Protein 13.7g 3%Vitamin A 25.4µg 0%Vitamin C 0mg 1%Calcium 7.7mg 2%Iron 0.4mg 0%Vitamin D 0µg 6%Magnesium 25mg 5%Potassium 233.2mg 5%Vitamin B6 0.1mg 67%Vitamin B12 1.6µg

Here's how to make your favorite restaurant style scallops at home: easy Pan Seared Scallops! Scallops have a beautiful, mild sweet flavor that's easy to love: and there's nothing better than that perfect seared crispy outside. But let's be straight about it. Scallops are easy to cook, but they're tricky to get right. It takes a little know how to get that golden brown crust without under cooking or overcooking them. But once you know a few secrets…it's very easy and takes only 5 minutes to cook. Here's everything you need to know about pan seared scallops…done right.

Easy Grain Bowl

Prep Time: 15 minutes
Cook Time: 15 minutes
Servings 4

Ingredients

For the grain bowl

- 2 15-ounce can chickpeas*
- 2 small garlic cloves
- 2 tablespoons olive oil
- ½ teaspoon smoked paprika or regular paprika
- 1 teaspoon kosher salt
- 1 recipe Tahini Sauce
- 1 pint cherry tomatoes
- 1 English cucumber
- ½ cup Kalamata olives (optional)
- 1/4 red onion

For the grain

- Seasoned Quinoa (shown here)
- White or Brown Rice (season like the quinoa)
- Farro
- Bulgur Wheat
- Millet
-

Preparation

1. **Make the grain:** Go to Seasoned Quinoa to make the quinoa, or follow the other whole grain recipes listed above. The quinoa takes about 25 minutes total, so use the cook time to prepare the remaining Ingredients.
2. **Make the chickpeas:** Drain and rinse the chickpeas. Mince the garlic. In a large skillet, heat the olive oil over medium heat. Add the garlic and sauté for 1 minute until fragrant but before it browns. Add the chickpeas, smoked paprika, salt, and several grinds of black pepper. Cook 2 minutes until warmed through.
3. **Make the sauce:** Make the Tahini Sauce. (Or, try Lemon Dill Sauce or Creamy Cilantro Sauce.)
4. **Prep the veggies:** Slice the tomatoes in half. Slice the cucumber. Slice the red onion.
5. **Assemble the bowls:** Place the quinoa and chickpeas in the bowl. Add the fresh veggies and drizzle with the sauce. (Meal prep notes: You can make quinoa, chickpeas, and dressing in advance: quinoa stores refrigerated 5 days and chickpeas store 3 to 4 days, and the dressing stores 1 month.)

Nutrition fact

Total Fat 30.1g Saturated Fat 4g 25%Total Carbohydrate 69.2g 55%Dietary Fiber 15.4g Sugars 3.9g 43%Protein 21.5g 4%Vitamin A 39.2µg 22%Vitamin C 20mg 12%Calcium 155.9mg 36%Iron 6.4mg 0%Vitamin D 0µg 42%Magnesium 177mg 19%Potassium 894.2mg 81%Vitamin B6 1.4mg 0%Vitamin B12 0µg

Easy Baked Shrimp

Prep Time: 10 minutes
Cook Time: 5 minutes
Servings 4

Ingredients

- 1 pound large shrimp, deveined (tail on or off)
- 2 tablespoons olive oil
- 2 garlic cloves
- ½ teaspoon dried oregano*
- ½ teaspoon onion powder
- ½ teaspoon kosher salt
- Lemon wedges
- Chopped parsley or cilantro, for garnish

Preparation

1. Preheat the oven to 400 degrees Fahrenheit or preheat the broiler.
2. If frozen, thaw the shrimp.
3. Mince the garlic. Pat the shrimp dry. In a medium bowl, toss with the shrimp with the olive oil, garlic, oregano, onion powder, and kosher salt.
4. Baked method: Line a baking sheet with parchment paper. Place the shrimp on a baking sheet in an even layer. Place the baking sheet in the oven and bake until juicy and opaque, about 4 to 6 minutes depending on the size of the shrimp.
5. Broiler method: Place the shrimp on a baking sheet in an even layer. Place the baking sheet in the broiler and broil for 3 to 6 minutes, until juicy and opaque, rotating the tray as necessary for even cooking.
6. Spritz with fresh lemon juice from lemon wedges, sprinkle with chopped parsley or cilantro, and serve immediately.

Nutrition fact

Total Fat 7.6g Saturated Fat 1.1g 0%Total Carbohydrate 0g 0%Dietary Fiber 0g Sugars 0g 46%Protein 22.8g 0%Vitamin A 0g 0%Vitamin C 0g 6%Calcium 72.5mg 3%Iron 0.6mg 0%Vitamin D 0g 9%Magnesium 39.7mg 6%Potassium 299.2mg 0%Vitamin B6 0g 0%Vitamin B12 0g

Shrimp is a big winner around here: it's delicious, a healthy lean protein, and so fast to cook. (And our 3 year old is obsessed.) Alex and my usual way to cook it is this sauteed shrimp. But the other day we thought: why not try baked shrimp in the oven? Well, you would not believe the "Wow's!" Exclaimed after every bite. This method is so easy and the shrimp come out juicy and perfectly seasoned with garlic and herbs. Move over, all other shrimp recipes! This one is the perfect healthy, fast and easy dinner.

Asparagus Risotto

Prep Time: 20 minutes
Cook Time: 15 minutes
Servings 4

Ingredients

- 1 quart vegetable broth
- 1 quart water
- 1 ½ teaspoons kosher salt, divided
- 1 pound asparagus
- 3 tablespoons extra-virgin olive oil, divided
- 1 lemon (Zest from half, plus 4 slices from the other half)
- 2 tablespoons salted butter
- 1/2 yellow onion
- ¼ teaspoon garlic powder
- 2 cups white arborio rice
- 1 cup dry white wine, such as Pinot Grigio or Chardonnay
- 1 cup shredded Parmesan cheese
- Freshly ground black pepper
- Optional garnish: Toasted pine nuts

Preparation

1. Preheat the oven to 425 degrees Fahrenheit.
2. **Heat the broth:** Combine the broth, water, and 1 teaspoon kosher salt in a saucepan and place it over low heat. (You'll use this warmed broth to stir into the risotto).
3. **Cut the vegetables:** Mince the onion, then place it in a bowl and reserve. Cut off the tough bottom ends of the asparagus and then cut them into two-inch pieces.
4. **Prep the asparagus:** Add the asparagus stalks to a parchment-lined baking sheet. Drizzle them with 1 tablespoon olive oil, then sprinkle on ½ teaspoon kosher salt and a few grinds of black pepper. Add the zest of ½ lemon and mix with your hands. Thinly slice 2 lemon wheels from the lemon, then cut each in half and add them right on the tray.
5. **Start the risotto:** Heat 2 tablespoons olive oil and the 2 tablespoons butter in a large skillet over medium heat. Add the minced onion and cook for 4 to 5 minutes until tender. Add the garlic powder and rice and cook, stirring occasionally, about 2 minutes until the rice starts to turn light brown. Stir in the wine and cook until the liquid is fully absorbed.
6. **Roast the asparagus:** Place the tray with the asparagus in the oven and 10 to 15 minutes, until bright green and tender when pierced by a fork at the thickest part. The timing will depend on the thickness of the asparagus spears. (You'll remove it from the oven while you're cooking the risotto in the next step.)
7. **Meanwhile, cook the risotto:** Add two ladles of the hot broth to the risotto. Cook, stirring occasionally until the liquid is fully absorbed, then add two more ladles of both. Cook in this same manner for about 12 minutes, adding two ladles and stirring. After the 12 minutes, taste a grain of rice. If it's creamy but still al dente in the center, you're ready for the final step! If not, continue to cook and add broth for a few minutes more.
8. **Finish the risotto:** When the rice is al dente, reduce the heat to low. Add two more ladles of broth, the Parmesan cheese and a few grinds of black pepper. Stir vigorously for 1 to 2 minutes until you've got a thick and creamy risotto. Then stir in the asparagus and roasted lemon wedges and serve immediately. Stores refrigerated in a sealed container for 3 days, though the color of the asparagus will fade (reheat before serving).

Italian Lentil Soup

Prep Time: 10 minutes
Cook Time: 30 minutes
Servings 6

Ingredients

- 1 large yellow onion
- 3 garlic cloves
- 1 15-ounce can quartered artichoke hearts
- ½ bunch Tuscan kale (also labeled as Lacinato, dinosaur kale or cavolo nero)
- 2 tablespoons olive oil
- 1 tablespoon dried oregano
- 1 tablespoon dried basil
- 1 cup dried red lentils
- 2 cups water
- 1 bay leaf
- ¼ teaspoon red pepper flakes
- 1 teaspoon kosher salt
- 2 28-ounce cans fire roasted whole tomatoes
- Shaved Parmesan cheese (optional), for garnish

Preparation

1. Dice the onion. Mince the garlic. Drain the artichoke hearts, and chop them into bite sized pieces. Wash and thinly slice the kale into ribbons.
2. In a large soup pot, heat the olive oil over medium heat and saute the onion for 5 minutes, until translucent. Add the minced garlic, dried oregano, and dried basil. Saute for another minute.
3. Add the red lentils, water, red pepper flakes, kosher salt, and 1 bay leaf and bring to a boil.
4. Once boiling, reduce to a simmer and add the kale, artichokes, and the liquid from the whole tomatoes. Then chop the whole tomatoes into bite sized pieces, and add them to the pot.
5. Simmer for 20 minutes, until the lentils are tender. Be careful not to overcook the lentils, or they will become too soft.
6. Taste, and additional kosher salt as necessary. Serve with a drizzle of olive oil and shaved Parmesan cheese.

Nutrition fact

Total Fat 5.4g Saturated Fat 0.9g 11%Total Carbohydrate 30.1g 24%Dietary Fiber 6.7g Sugars 4g 19%Protein 9.3g 4%Vitamin A 32.9µg 10%Vitamin C 9.4mg 5%Calcium 62mg 17%Iron 3mg 0%Vitamin D 0µg 7%Magnesium 30mg 136%Potassium 6400.1mg 15%Vitamin B6 0.3mg 0%Vitamin B12 0µg

Best Chickpea Burgers

Prep Time: 14 minutes
Cook Time: 26 minutes
Servings 4

Ingredients

For the chickpea burgers*
- 15-ounce can chickpeas (1 ½ cups cooked)
- 1 large carrot
- ½ red onion
- 2 garlic cloves
- ¼ cup all purpose, whole wheat or gluten-free flour
- 2 tablespoons tahini
- 1 teaspoon cumin
- 2 teaspoons smoked paprika
- 1 teaspoon kosher salt
- ½ teaspoon black pepper
- ¼ cup grapeseed or vegetable oil, for frying

For serving
- Your favorite BBQ sauce (optional; check the label to find an organic version without high fructose corn syrup)
- Lettuce, tomato and red onion
- Shiitake bacon (optional but recommended!)
- Spicy Mayo or Special Burger Sauce
- 4 burger buns

Preparation

1. Preheat the oven to 400°F.
2. Drain and rinse the chickpeas. Use a potato masher or fork to mash them in a bowl until they're mostly mashed with some chunks. Use a large size grater to grate the onion and carrot, then finely grate the garlic OR place them all in a food processor and process until finely minced. Add them to the bowl with the chickpeas. Stir in the tahini, flour and spices. Mix with a spoon and then your fingers until a sticky dough forms. Form 4 round patties and place them on a cutting board, about 3 inches wide by about ¾ inch thick (we had a 3-inch circle biscuit cutter, which you could use if you have one).
3. In a medium frying pan, heat ¼ cup oil over medium heat. Carefully add the patties to the pan. If you have one, top with a splatter screen. Fry for about 3 to 4 minutes until golden brown on one side. Flip and fry for another 3 to 4 minutes until golden brown, turning down the heat as necessary.
4. Transfer the patties to a parchment lined baking sheet. Bake for 20 minutes until golden brown and baked through.
5. Remove the patties from the oven and let them cool for at least 15 minutes to firm up. Paint liberally with BBQ sauce. Top with toppings (make sure to have a creamy rich topping like the Spicy Mayo or Special Sauce to enhance the flavors and textures. The burgers save well in the refrigerator, so they're great to make ahead and eat throughout the week. They also freeze well!

Nutrition fact

Total Fat 19.8g Saturated Fat 11.9g 9%Total Carbohydrate 26g 22%Dietary Fiber 6.2g Sugars 2.5g 15%Protein 7.4g 33%Vitamin A 297µg 5%Vitamin C 4.3mg 5%Calcium 69mg 14%Iron 2.6mg 0%Vitamin D 0µg 10%Magnesium 43.3mg 7%Potassium 345.7mg 33%Vitamin B6 0.6mg 0%Vitamin B12 0µg

Easy Hummus Recipe (Authentic and Homemade)

Prep Time: 5 minutes
Cook Time: 15 minutes
Servings   8

Ingredients

- 3 cups cooked chickpeas, peeled (from 1 to 1 ¼ cup dry chickpeas or from quality canned chickpeas. See recipe notes for more instructions on cooking and peeling chickpeas)
- 1 to 2 garlic cloves, minced
- 3 to 4 ice cubes
- ⅓ cup   (79 grams) tahini paste
- ½ tsp kosher salt
- Juice of 1 lemon
- Hot water (if needed)
- Early Harvest Greek extra virgin olive oil
- Sumac

Preparation

1. Add chickpeas and minced garlic to the bowl of a food processor. Puree until a smooth, powder-like mixture forms.
2. While processor is running, add ice cubes, tahini, salt, and lemon juice. Blend for about 4 minutes or so. Check, and if the consistency is too thick still, run processor and slowly add a little hot water. Blend until you reach desired silky smooth consistency.
3. Spread in a serving bowl and add a generous drizzle of Early Harvest EVOO. Add a few chickpeas to the middle, if you like. Sprinkle sumac on top. Enjoy with warm pita wedges and your favorite veggies.

How to make hummus the traditional way. No fuss. No extra flavors added. Just a plain, classic homemade hummus recipe. And a couple of tricks will ensure you achieve the best hummus ever--thick, smooth, rich, and ultra creamy. Be sure to see the video tutorial as well.

Nutrition Facts

Serves 8 Amount Per Serving Calories 176 % Daily Value* Total Fat 8.7g 11% Saturated Fat 1.2g Trans Fat 0g Sodium 153.2mg 7% Total Carbohydrate 19.4g 7% Sugars 3.1g Protein 7.2 14% Vitamin C3%Calcium3%Iron12%Vitamin D0%Magnesium9%Potassium5%Zinc13%Phosphorus15%Thiamin (B1)19%Riboflavin (B2)4%Niacin (B3)6%Vitamin B66%Folic Acid (B9)29%Vitamin E1%Vitamin K3%

Easy Sheet Pan Baked Eggs and Vegetables

Prep Time: 5 minutes
Cook Time: 15 minutes
Servings 6

Ingredients

- 1 green bell pepper, cored and thinly sliced
- 1 orange bell pepper, cored and thinly sliced
- 1 red bell pepper, cored and thinly sliced
- 1 medium red onion, halved then thinly sliced
- Kosher salt and black pepper
- Spices of your choice, I used 2 teaspoon za'atar blend, 1 teaspoon ground cumin and 1 teaspoon Aleppo chili pepper
- Extra virgin olive oil, I used Early Harvest Greek extra virgin olive oil
- 6 large eggs
- Chopped fresh parsley, a large handful
- 1 Roma tomato, diced
- Crumbled feta, a small bit to your liking (optional)

Preparation

1. Preheat the oven to 400 degrees F.
2. Place sliced bell peppers (all colors) in a large mixing bowl. Add red onions. Season with kosher salt and pepper, 1 teaspoon za'atar, 1 teaspoon cumin and 1 teaspoon Aleppo chili pepper (keep the remaining za'atar for later). Drizzle with extra virgin olive oil. Toss to coat.
3. Transfer the pepper and onion medley to a large sheet pan. Spread in one layer. Bake in heated oven for 10 to 15 minutes.
4. Remove pan from oven briefly. Carefully make 6 "holes" or openings among the roasted veggies. Carefully crack each egg into a hole, keeping the yoke intact (it helps to crack the egg in a small dish to slide carefully into each hole.)
5. Return pan to oven and bake until the egg whites settle. Watch the yokes to see them turn to the doness you like (anywhere from 5 to 8 minutes).
6. Remove from oven. Season eggs to your liking. Sprinkle remaining 1 teaspoon za'atar all over. Add parsley, diced tomatoes, and a sprinkle of feta. Serve immediately!

Nutrition fact

Calories: 142.7kcal Carbohydrates: 6g Protein: 7.2g Fat: 10.3g Saturated Fat: 2.8g Polyunsaturated Fat: 1.4g Monounsaturated Fat: 5.3g Trans Fat: 0.1g Cholesterol: 168.7mg Sodium: 227.5mg Potassium: 234mg Fiber: 1.6g Sugar: 3.4g Vitamin A: 1663.3IU Vitamin C: 69.5mg Calcium: 62.7mg Iron: 1.1mg

Healthy Breakfast Egg Muffins

Prep Time: 15 minutes
Cook Time: 25 minutes
Servings 12

Ingredients

- Extra virgin olive oil for brushing
- 1 small red bell pepper, chopped (about ¾ cup)
- 12 cherry tomatoes, halved
- 1 shallot, finely chopped
- 6 to 10 pitted kalamata olives, chopped
- 3 to 4 oz/113 g cooked chicken or turkey, boneless, shredded
- 1 oz/ 28. 34 g (about ½ cup) chopped fresh parsley leaves
- Handful crumbled feta to your liking
- 8 large eggs
- Salt and Pepper
- ½ tsp Spanish paprika
- ¼ tsp ground turmeric (optional)

Preparation

1. Place a rack in the center of your oven and preheat to 350 degrees F.
2. Prepare a 12-cup muffin pan like this one (or 12 individual muffin cups). Brush with extra virgin olive oil.
3. Divide the peppers, tomatoes, shallots, olives, chicken (or turkey), parsley, and crumbled feta among the 12 cups (they should come up to about ⅔ of the way full.)
4. In a large measuring cup or a mixing bowl, add eggs, salt, pepper, and spices. Whisk well to combine.
5. Pour the egg mixture carefully over each cup, leaving a little room at the top (should be about ¾ of the way or so.)
6. Place muffin pan or muffin cups on top of a sheet pan (to help catch any spills). Bake in heated oven for about 25 minutes or until the egg muffins are set.
7. Let cool for a few minutes, then run a small butter knife around the edges of each muffin to loosen. Remove from pan and serve!

Easy and healthy breakfast egg muffins. These low-crab, freezer friendly egg muffins make a great breakfast on the go! Also perfect for your next brunch, serve along with salad and other Mediterranean favorites (see notes for ideas!)

Nutrition Facts

Amount Per Serving Calories 67 % Daily Value* Total Fat 4.7g 6% Sodium 161.4mg 7% Total Carbohydrate 1.2g 0% Sugars 0.7g rotein 4.6g 9% Vitamin A9%Vitamin C17%Calcium2%Iron5%Vitamin D7%Magnesium2%Potassium2%Zinc5%Phosphorus6%Thiamin (B1)2%Riboflavin (B2)14%Niacin (B3)1%Vitamin B66%Folic Acid (B9)6%Vitamin B1213%Vitamin E3%Vitamin K52%

Ful Mudammas (Egyptian Fava Beans)

Prep Time: 15 minutes
Cook Time: 10 minutes
Servings 5

Ingredients

- 2 cans plain fava beans (13 to 15 ounces each can) (see notes if using dry fava beans)
- ½ cup water
- Kosher salt
- ½ to 1 teaspoon ground cumin
- 1 to 2 hot peppers, chopped (jalapenos will work here)
- 2 garlic cloves, chopped
- 1 large lemon juice of
- Extra virgin olive oil (Early Harvest)
- 1 cup chopped parsley
- 1 tomato, diced

To Serve:

- Warm pit bread
- Sliced tomatoes
- Sliced cucumbers
- Green onions
- Olives

Preparation

1. In a cast iron skillet or saucepan, add the fava beans and ½ cup water. Warm over medium-high heat. Season with kosher salt and cumin. Use a potato masher or fork to mash the fava beans.
2. In a morter and pestle, add the hot peppers and garlic. Smash. Add in juice of one lemon and stir to combine.
3. Pour the garlic and hot pepper sauce over the fava beans. Add a generous drizzle of extra virgin olive oil. Top with chopped parsley, diced tomatoes, and a few slices of hot peppers, if you like.
4. Serve with pita bread, sliced veggies and olives.

Foul mudammas recipe, made with hearty, creamy fava beans and loaded with flavor from ground cumin, fresh herbs, and a zippy lemon garlic sauce with hot peppers! Don't worry, the sauce is not spicy, but it adds just the right kick.
I use a shortcut in this quick fava beans recipe. Serve it with warm pita bread and sliced veggies. Or turn it into a big vegan feast with falafel and sides like tahini, hummus, and roasted cauliflower!

Nutrition Facts

Amount Per Serving Calories 154 % Daily Value* Total Fat 3.5g 4% Sodium 10.6mg 0% Total Carbohydrate 22.3g 8% sugars 9.6g Protein 0.9g   2% Vitamin A7%Vitamin C41%Calcium4%Iron18%Magnesium3%Potassium4%Zinc2%Phosphorus2%Thiamin (B1)3%Riboflavin (B2)2%Niacin (B3)3%Vitamin B66%Folic Acid (B9)7%Vitamin B120%Vitamin E2%Vitamin K251%

The Ultimate Mediterranean Breakfast

Prep Time: 30 minutes
Cook Time: 30 minutes
Servings 6-12

Ingredients

- 1 Falafel Recipe
- 1 Classic Hummus Recipe (or roasted garlic hummus, roasted red pepper hummus)
- 1 Baba Ganoush Recipe
- Feta cheese or 1 Labneh Recipe
- 1 Tabouli Recipe
- 1 to 2 tomatoes, sliced
- 1 English cucumber, sliced
- 6 to 7 Radish, halved or sliced
- Assorted olives (I like a mix of green olives and kalamata olives)
- Marinated artichokes or mushrooms
- Early Harvest EVOO and Za'atar to dip
- Pita Bread, sliced into quarters
- Grapes (palette cleanser)
- Fresh herbs for garnish

Preparation

1. Note: Plan to make most of these ahead of time for quick and easy assembly. See notes.
2. **Make the falafel according to this recipe.** You will need to begin at least the night before to soak the chickpeas. See notes below for working ahead. (You may also buy falafel at a local Middle Eastern store.)
3. **Make the hummus according to this recipe,** and Baba ganoush according to this recipe. You can prepare both of these the night before and store in the fridge. If you like, try roasted garlic hummus or roasted red pepper hummus to change things up. (If you don't have the time, use quality store-bought hummus.)
4. **Slice feta cheese,** or prepare Labneh ahead of time according to this recipe.
5. **Make tabouli according to this recipe.** Can be made a couple days in advance and refrigerated in tight-lid glass containers.
6. **To assemble the Mediterranean breakfast board,** place the hummus, baba ganoush, olive oil, za'atar, tabouli in bowls. Place the largest bowl in the center of a large wooden board or platter to create a focal point. Arrange the remaining bowls on different parts of the board or platter to create movement and shape. Use the gaps between the bowls to place the remaining Ingredients like falafel, sliced vegetables, and pita bread. Add grapes and garnish with fresh herbs, if you like.
7. A Mediterranean diet breakfast is every bit as wholesome and satisfying as it is delicious. My favorite way to serve a crowd is this Mediterranean brunch board showcasing savory, nutrition-packed favorites like falafel, hummus, baba ganoush and tabouli. Many of these items can be prepared ahead and easily assembled when you need them (see recipe notes.) Be sure to read the full post for more breakfast ideas!

3-Ingredient Mediterranean Salad

Prep Time:	10 minutes
Cook Time:	0 minutes
Servings	4

Ingredients

- 6 Roma tomatoes, diced (about 3 cups diced tomatoes)
- 1 Large English cucumber, or hot-house cucumber, diced
- ½ to ¾ cup chopped fresh parsley leaves
- Kosher salt, to taste
- ½ teaspoon black pepper
- 1 teaspoon ground Sumac
- 2 tablespoon extra virgin olive oil, try a robust like Greek Early Harvest or Hojiblanca Spanish EVOO
- 2 teaspoon freshly squeezed lemon juice

Preparation

1. In a large mixing bowl, place the diced tomatoes, cucumbers, and parsley. Season with kosher salt and toss. Set aside for 5 minutes or so.
2. Add the sumac, olive oil, and lemon juice. Give the salad a gentle toss. Enjoy!

Easy all-star Mediterranean salad with three star Ingredients: tomatoes, cucumbers, and parsley, seasoned simply and dressed in extra virgin olive oil and lemon juice! You'll love this everyday cucumber and tomato salad next to your favorite Mediterranean entrees. You can change it up by adding feta cheese, chickpeas, or even a cup of cooked couscous to turn it into a meal!

Nutrition fact

Calories: 62.5kcal Carbohydrates: 4.8g Protein: 1g Fat: 4.9g Saturated Fat: 0.7g Polyunsaturated Fat: 0.6g Monounsaturated Fat: 3.4g Sodium: 7mg Potassium: 252.1mg Fiber: 1.2g Sugar: 2.6g Vitamin A: 991.2IU Vitamin C: 17.2mg Calcium: 22mg Iron: 0.7mg

10-Minute Citrus Avocado Salsa (Chunky Avocado Dip)

Prep Time: 10 minutes
Cook Time: 0 minutes
Servings 6

Ingredients

- 2 Navel oranges, peeled and diced
- 2 large avocados, or 3 smaller avocados, pitted, peeled and diced
- ½ cup chopped red onions
- ½ cup chopped cilantro
- ½ cup chopped fresh mint
- ½ cup walnuts, chopped
- Salt and pepper
- ¾ teaspoon Sumac
- ½ teaspoon Cayenne pepper, or to your liking
- Juice of 1 lime
- Extra virgin olive oil
- 1 to 2 tablespoons crumbled feta cheese

Preparation

1. Place oranges, avocado, red onions, fresh herbs, and walnuts in one large bowl. Season with salt, pepper, sumac and pinch of cayenne.
2. Add lime juice and a generous drizzle of extra virgin olive oil. Toss gently to combine. Add feta cheese on top. Serve with your favorite healthy chips

This chunky citrus avocado dip borrows a bit of a Mediterranean twist that will surprise your taste buds in the best way. With oranges, walnuts, feta, and fresh herbs, this avocado salsa is satisfying and delicious. It's a good one for guacamole lovers who are looking for something different! Just add pita chips or serve with your favorite chips or crackers. More ideas in the notes.

Nutrition fact

Calories: 208kcal Carbohydrates: 15g Protein: 4.1g Fat: 16.6g Saturated Fat: 2.2g Monounsaturated Fat: 7.5g Cholesterol: 1.3mg Sodium: 30mg Potassium: 496.5mg Fiber: 6.8g Sugar: 5.3g Vitamin A: 533.9IU Vitamin C: 37.1mg Calcium: 51mg Iron: 1mg

Quick Roasted Tomatoes with Garlic And Thyme

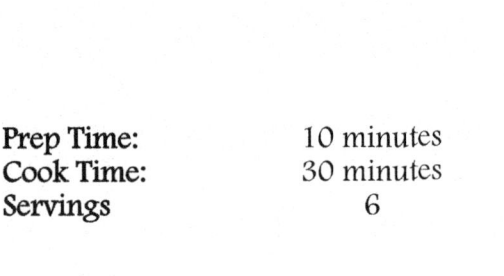

Prep Time: 10 minutes
Cook Time: 30 minutes
Servings 6

Ingredients

- 2 lb Smaller Tomatoes, halved (I used Campari tomatoes)
- 2 to 3 garlic cloves, minced
- Kosher salt and black pepper
- 2 teaspoon fresh thyme, stems removed
- 1 teaspoon sumac
- ½ teaspoon dry chili pepper flakes, I used Aleppo Pepper which is milder
- Extra virgin olive oil, I used Private Reserve Greek extra virgin olive oil
- Crumbled feta cheese/ anchovies, optional

Preparation

1. Preheat the oven to 450 degrees F.
2. Place the tomato halves in a large mixing bowl. Add minced garlic, salt, pepper, fresh thyme, and spices. Drizzle a generous amount, about ¼ cup or more, quality extra virgin olive. Toss to coat.
3. Transfer the tomatoes to a baking sheet with a rim. Spread the tomatoes in one single layer, flesh side up.
4. Roast in your heated oven for 30 to 35 minutes or until the tomatoes have collapsed to your desired doneness.
5. Remove from heat. If you are planning to serve it soon, feel free to garnish with more fresh thyme and a few sprinkles of feta cheese. Enjoy warm or at room temperature.

Tomatoes, tossed with garlic, fresh thyme, and spices, then roasted in a high-heated oven until super tender and bursting with intense, concentrated flavor. There are so many ways to use up roasted tomatoes-~as a delicious side; tossed in pasta or soup; or served bruschetta-style on top of your favorite toasted bread.   Heck, you can serve them with homemade pita chips.

Nutrition fact

Calories: 30.4kcal Carbohydrates: 5.6g Protein: 1.4g Fat: 0.5g Saturated Fat: 0.1g Sodium: 201.5mg Potassium: 358.3mg Fiber: 1.8g Sugar: 4g Vitamin A: 1272.1iun   Vitamin C: 21.5mg Calcium: 16.9mg Iron: 0.5mg

Roasted Cauliflower and Chickpea Stew

Prep Time: 10 minutes
Cook Time: 50 minutes
Servings 6

Ingredients

- 1 ½ tsp ground turmeric
- 1 ½ tsp ground cumin
- 1 ½ tsp ground cinnamon
- 1 tsp ground coriander
- 1 tsp Sweet paprika
- 1 tsp cayenne pepper (optional)
- ½ tsp ground green cardamom
- 1 whole head cauliflower, divided into small florets
- 5 medium-sized bulk carrots, peeled, cut into 1 ½" pieces
- Salt and pepper
- Private Reserve extra virgin olive oil
- 1 large sweet onion, chopped
- 6 garlic cloves, chopped
- 2 14-oz cans chickpeas, drained and rinsed
- 1 28-oz can diced tomatoes with its juice
- ½ cup parsley leaves, stems removed, roughly chopped
- Toasted slivered almonds (optional)
- Toasted pine nuts (optional)

Preparation

1. Preheat the oven to 475 degrees F.
2. In a small bowl, mix together the spices.
3. Place the cauliflower florets and carrot pieces on a large lightly oiled baking sheet. Season with salt and pepper. Add a little more than ½ of the spice mixture. Drizzle generously with olive oil, then toss to make sure the spices evenly coat the cauliflower and carrots.
4. Bake in the 475 degrees F heated-oven for 20 minutes or until the carrots and cauliflower soften and gain some color. Remove from the heat and set aside for now. Turn the oven off.
5. In a large cast iron pot or Dutch oven, heat 2 tablespoon olive oil. Add the onions and saute for 3 minutes, then add the garlic and the remaining spices. Cook on medium-high for 2-3 more minutes, stirring constantly.
6. Now add the chickpeas and canned tomatoes. Season with salt and pepper. Stir in the roasted cauliflower and carrots. Bring everything to a boil, then reduce the heat to medium-low, cover part-way and cook for another 20 minutes. Be sure to check the stew, stir occasionally, and add a little water if needed.
7. Remove from the heat and transfer to serving bowls. Garnish with fresh parsley and the toasted nuts (optional.) Enjoy hot over some quick-cooked couscous or with a side of warm pita bread.

Nutrition Facts

Amount Per Serving Calories 286 % Daily Value* Total Fat 12.5g 16% Saturated Fat 1.6g Trans Fat 0g Total Carbohydrate 37.1g 13% Dietary Fiber 13.2g 47% Sugars 8.6g Protein 11g 22% Vitamin A61%Vitamin C53%Calcium14 Iron24%Magnesium21%Potassium20%Zinc16%Phosphorus17%Thiamin (B1)74 Riboflavin (B2)21%Niacin (B3)15%Vitamin B661%Folic Acid (B9)23%Vitamin E18%Vitamin K60%

Easy White Bean Salad

Prep Time: 15 minutes
Cook Time: 15 minutes
Servings 4

Ingredients

- 2 cans white beans (cannellini), drained and rinsed well
- 1 English cucumber, diced
- 10 oz grape or cherry tomatoes, halved
- 4 green onions, chopped
- 1 cup chopped fresh parsley
- 15 to 20 mint leaves, chopped
- 1 lemon, zested and juiced
- Salt and pepper
- Spices (1 teaspoon Za'atar and ½ teaspoon each Sumac and Aleppo. See notes for more options)
- Extra virgin olive oil (I used Early Harvest EVOO)
- Feta cheese, optional

Preparation

1. Add white beans, cucumbers, tomatoes, green onions, parsley and mint to a large mixing bowl.
2. Add lemon zest. Season with salt and pepper, then add za'atar, sumac and Aleppo pepper.
3. Finish with lemon juice and a generous drizzle of extra virgin olive oil (2 to 3 tablespoons). Give the salad a good toss to combine. Taste and adjust seasoning. Add feta cheese, if you like. (For best flavor, let the salad sit in the dressing for 30 minutes or so before serving. See notes).

Simple white bean salad loaded with bright Mediterranean flavors! Canned beans, chopped veggies, and fresh herbs tossed together in one big bowl. No fancy dressing here, a squeeze of lemon juice and extra virgin olive oil is all you need. Prepare it ahead for best flavor (see notes).

Nutrition Facts

Calories 205 % Daily Value* Total Fat 6g   8% Sodium 679mg   30% Total Carbohydrate 31.4g 11% Sugars 5.8g Protein 9.7g 19% Vitamin A14%Vitamin C62%Calcium9%Iron21%Vitamin D0%Magnesium24%Potassium8%Zinc22%Phosphorus14%Thiamin (B1)76%Riboflavin (B2)19%Niacin (B3)5%Vitamin B68%Folic Acid (B9)21%Vitamin B122%Vitamin E4%Vitamin K345%

Mediterranean Watermelon Salad Recipe

Prep Time: 15 minutes
Cook Time: 15 minutes
Servings 4

Ingredients

For The Honey-Lime Dressing

- 2 tablespoon honey
- 2 tablespoon lime juice
- 1 to 2 tablespoon quality extra virgin olive oil I used Greek Early Harvest
- Pinch of salt

For The Watermelon Salad

- ½ watermelon peeled, cut into cubes
- 1 English or Hot House cucumber, cubed (about 2 cupfuls of cubed cucumbers)
- 15 fresh mint leaves chopped
- 15 fresh basil leaves chopped
- ½ cup crumbled feta cheese more to your liking

Preparation

1. Make the dressing. In a small bowl, whisk together the honey, lime juice, olive oil and pinch of salt. Set aside for a moment.
2. Make the Salad. In a large bowl or serving platter with sides, combine the watermelon, cucumbers, and fresh herbs.
3. Top the watermelon salad with the dressing and gently toss to combine. Top with the feta cheese and serve!

This simple and refreshing watermelon salad is made of sweet watermelon, cucumbers, creamy salty feta, fresh mint and basil. The lime-honey dressing brings this salad together, adding tang and a little extra punch. This salad is best prepared and served right away, but you can make the dressing up to 3 days in advance and save it in the fridge.

Traditional Greek Salad

Prep Time: 15 minutes
Cook Time: 15 minutes
Servings 6

Ingredients

- 1 medium red onion
- 4 Medium juicy tomatoes
- 1 English cucumber (hot house cucumber) partially peeled making a striped pattern
- 1 green bell pepper cored
- Greek pitted Kalamata olives a handful to your liking
- Kosher salt a pinch
- 4 tablespoon quality extra virgin olive oil I used Early Harvest Greek olive oil
- 1-2 tablespoon red wine vinegar
- Blocks of Greek feta cheese do not crumble the feta, leave it in large pieces
- ½ tablespoon dried oregano

Preparation

1. Cut the red onion in half and thinly slice into half moons. (If you want to take the edge off, place the sliced onions in a solution of iced water and vinegar for a bit before adding to the salad. I do this in the video).
2. Cut the tomatoes into wedges or large chunks (I sliced some into rounds and cut the rest in wedges).
3. Cut the partially peeled cucumber in half length-wise, then slice into thick halves (at least ½" in thickness)
4. Thinly slice the bell pepper into rings.
5. Place everything in a large salad dish. Add a good handful of pitted kalamata olives.
6. Season very lightly with kosher salt (just a pinch) and a bit of dried oregano.
7. Pour the olive oil and red wine vinegar all over the salad. Give everything a very gentle toss to mix (do NOT over mix, this salad is not meant to be handled too much).
8. Now add the the feta blocks on top and add a sprinkle more of dried oregano.
9. Serve with crusty bread.

Nutrition Fact

Calories: 102.9kcal Carbohydrates: 4.7g Protein: 0.7g Fat: 9.5g Saturated Fat: 1.3g Sodium: 2.8mg Potassium: 135mg Fiber: 1.1g Vitamin A: 125.9IU Vitamin C: 18.7mg Calcium: 20.9mg Iron: 0.5mg

Baked Zucchini with Parmesan and Thyme

Prep Time: 10 minutes
Cook Time: 15 minutes
Servings 5

Ingredients

- 3 to 4 zucchini trimmed and cut length-wise into quarters (sticks)
- Extra virgin olive oil I used Private Reserve Greek extra virgin olive oil

For Parmesan-Thyme Topping:

- ½ cup grated Parmesan cheese
- 2 teaspoon fresh thyme leaves no stems
- 1 teaspoon dried oregano
- ½ teaspoon sweet paprika I used this all-natural paprika
- ½ teaspoon black pepper
- Pinch kosher salt

Preparation

1. Heat oven to 350 degrees F.
2. In a bowl, mix together the grated Parmesan, thyme and spices until well combined.
3. Prepare a large baking sheet topped with a wire baking rack like this one. Lightly brush the baking rack with extra virgin olive oil (or use a healthy cooking spray.) Arrange the zucchini sticks, skin-side down, on the baking rack and brush each zucchini stick with extra virgin olive oil
4. Sprinkle the Parmesan-thyme topping on each zucchini stick
5. Bake in heated oven for 15 to 20 minutes or until tender. Then, for a golden crispy topping, broil for 2 to 3 minutes more, watching carefully.
6. Serve immediately as an appetizer with a side of tzatziki or hummus for dipping! Or serve it as a side next to your protein of choice.

Nutrition Fact

Calories: 66kcal Carbohydrates: 4.8g Protein: 5.4g Fat: 3.3g Saturated Fat: 1.8g Potassium: 319.4mg Fiber: 1.6g Vitamin A: 458.2IU Vitamin C: 22.3mg Calcium: 139.3mg Iron: 0.9mg

Easy Baba Ganoush Recipe

Prep Time: 15 minutes
Cook Time: 20 minutes
Servings 4

Ingredients

- 2 Italian eggplants or small globe eggplants
- ¼ cup tahini paste I used Soom tahini
- 1 lemon, juice of
- 1 garlic clove, minced
- 1 tablespoon plain Greek yogurt, optional
- Kosher salt and black pepper
- 1 teaspoon sumac
- ¾ teaspoon Aleppo pepper or red pepper flakes, optional
- Extra virgin olive oil
- Toasted pine nuts for garnish, optional

Preparation

1. First, smoke or grill the eggplant. Turn one gas burner on medium-high. Place the eggplant directly over the flame. Using a pair of tongs, turn the eggplant every 5 minutes or so until it is tender and the skin is charred and crispy on all sides (20 minutes.) The eggplant should deflate and become super tender. Supposed to. If you don't have a gas burner you can use a grill. You can also roast the eggplant in the oven (see notes).
2. Remove the eggplant from the heat and transfer it to a large colander over a bowl. Allow it to sit and drain for a few minutes until fully cooled and all excess water has been drained (it helps if you open the eggplant up a bit and push on it with a knife or a spoon to help it release its juices).
3. Once the eggplant is cool enough to touch, peel the charred crispy skin off (it should come right off). Discard the skin and the stem (don't worry if a few bits of the skin remain, that is just added flavor).
4. Transfer the cooked and fully drained eggplant to a bowl. Use a fork to break it down into smaller pieces. Add the tahini paste, garlic, lemon juice, Greek yogurt (if using) salt, pepper, sumac, Aleppo pepper or crushed red pepper flakes. Mix gently with a wooden spoon or a fork until well-combined.
5. Cover the baba ganoush and chill in the fridge for 30 minutes to an hour.
6. To serve, transfer the baba ganoush to a rimmed serving dish or a bowl. Top with a good drizzle of extra virgin olive oil and toasted pine nuts, if you like. Serve with pita wedges or pita chips and veggies of your choice!

Nutrition Fact

Calories: 86.6kcal Carbohydrates: 8.6g Protein: 3g Fat: 5.6g Saturated Fat: 0.8g Monounsaturated Fat: 2g Cholesterol: 0.1mg Sodium: 204.4mg Potassium: 250.2mg Fiber: 3.3g Vitamin A: 103.6IU Vitamin C: 11.8mg Calcium: 30.3mg Iron: 0.8mg

Homemade Fish Sticks

Prep Time: 15 minutes
Cook Time: 20 minutes
Servings 4

Ingredients

- 1 ½ lb firm fish fillet such as salmon, skin removed (You can use a firm white fish fillet like cod)
- Salt
- 1 tsp black pepper
- 1 tsp dried oregano
- 1 tsp sweet paprika
- ½ cup flour (all-purpose, whole wheat or gluten free flour)
- 1 egg, beaten with 1 tablespoon water (egg wash)
- ½ cup bread crumbs
- ½ cup Parmesan
- Extra virgin olive oil (I used Private Reserve Greek EVOO)
- Zest of 1 lemon and juice of ½ lemon to finish
- Parsley for garnish

To serve:

- Tahini sauce or Tzatziki sauce

Preparation

1. Heat your oven to 450 degrees F.
2. Pat fish fillet dry and season with kosher salt on both sides. Cut the fish fillet into pieces or sticks (1 to 1 ½-inch thick and about 3-inch long).
3. In a small bowl, combine black pepper, dried oregano, and paprika. Season fish sticks on both sides with the spice mixture.
4. Make a dredging station. Place flour in a shallow dish. Place the egg wash in a deeper dish or bowl next to the flour dish. And in another dish, combine the bread crumbs, grated Parmesan and lemon zest. Place next to the dish with the egg wash.
5. Now coat the fish. Take a fish stick and dip it in the flour to coat both sides; shake excess flour off. Then dip the fish stick in the egg wash, and then in the bread crumb and Parmesan mixture. Pat to help the coating adhere to the fish stick. Repeat until all the fish sticks have been coated.
6. Arrange coated fish sticks on an oiled baking sheet. Brush the tops of the fish sticks with a little extra virgin olive oil (you'll want to basically dab the salmon fish sticks with the oil so that you don't end up removing the coating).
7. Place the baking sheet on the middle rack of the heated oven. Bake for about 12 to 15 minutes. If the fish sticks need more color still, place them under the broiler very briefly (watch carefully) until fish sticks gain a nice golden brown color.
8. Finish with lemon zest and fresh lemon juice. Garnish with parsley.
9. Serve with your favorite sauce for dipping. I used tahini sauce here, but tzatziki sauce would be great as well. Add a big salad and call it dinner (I especially like Mediterranean white bean salad or Greek salad with these salmon fish sticks

Easy Homemade Chicken Shawarma

Prep Time: 10 minutes
Cook Time: 30 minutes
Servings 6

Ingredients

- ¾ tbsp ground cumin
- ¾ tbsp turmeric powder
- ¾ tbsp ground coriander
- ¾ tbsp garlic powder
- ¾ tbsp paprika
- ½ tsp ground cloves
- ½ tsp cayenne pepper, more if you prefer
- Salt
- 8 boneless, skinless chicken thighs
- 1 large onion, thinly sliced
- 1 large lemon, juice of
- ⅓ cup Private Reserve extra virgin olive oil

To Serve

- 6 pita pockets
- Tahini sauce or Greek Tzatziki sauce
- Baby arugula
- 3-ingredient Mediterranean Salad
- Pickles or kalmata olives (optional)

Preparation

1. In a small bowl, mix the cumin, turmeric, coriander, garlic powder, sweet paprika and cloves. Set aside the shawarma spice mix for now.
2. Pat the chicken thighs dry and season with salt on both sides, then thinly slice into small bite-sized pieces.
3. Place the chicken in a large bowl. Add the shwarma spices and toss to coat. Add the onions, lemon juice and olive oil. Toss everything together again. Cover and refrigerate for 3 hours or overnight (if you don't have time, you can cut or skip marinating time)
4. When ready, preheat the oven to 425 degrees F. Take the chicken out of the fridge and let it sit in room temperature for a few minutes.
5. Spread the marinated chicken with the onions in one layer on a large lightly-oiled baking sheet pan. Roast for 30 minutes in the 425 degrees F heated-oven. For a more browned, crispier chicken, move the pan to the top rack and broil very briefly (watch carefully). Remove from the oven.
6. While the chicken is roasting, prepare the pita pockets. Make tahini sauce according to this recipe or Tztaziki sauce according to this recipe. Make 3-ingredient Mediterranean salad according to this recipe. Set aside.
7. To serve, open pita pockets up. Spread a little tahini sauce or Tzatziki sauce, add chicken shawarma, arugula, Mediterranean salad and pickles or olives, if you like. Serve immediately!

Easy Greek Red Lentil Soup

Prep Time: 10 minutes
Cook Time: 23 minutes
Servings 6

Ingredients

- Extra virgin olive oil (I used Early Harvest)
- 1 large onion, chopped
- 3 garlic cloves, minced
- 2 carrots, chopped
- 3 tsp dry oregano
- 1 ½ tsp cumin
- 1 tsp rosemary
- ½ tsp red pepper flakes
- 2 dry bay leaves
- 1 cup crushed tomatoes (from a can)
- 7 cups low-sodium vegetable broth
- 2 cups red lentils, rinsed and drained
- Kosher salt
- Zest of 1 lemon
- Juice of 2 lemons
- Fresh parsley for garnish
- Crumbled feta cheese to serve, optional

Preparation

1. Heat 3 tablespoon extra virgin olive oil until shimmering but not smoking. Add onions, carrots and garlic. Cook 3 to 4 minutes, stirring regularly. Add spices and bay leaves. Cook for a few seconds till fragrant, keep stirring so spices don't burn.
2. Add crushed tomatoes, broth, lentils. Season with kosher salt. Bring to a boil, then lower heat to simmer for 15 to 20 minutes, until lentils are fully cooked.
3. Remove from heat. If you have the time, let soup cool a bit before using an immersion blender to puree. Pulse a few times till you reach the creamy consistency you are looking for.
4. Return soup to heat, and stir to warm through. Add lemon zest, lemon juice, and fresh parsley.
5. Transfer soup to serving bowls and top with extra virgin olive oil. If you like, top each bowl with a generous sprinkle of feta cheese. Serve with your favorite crusty bread!

Easy Salmon Soup

Prep Time: 10 minutes
Cook Time: 12 minutes
Servings 4

Ingredients

- Extra virgin olive oil (I used Private Reserve Greek EVOO)
- 4 green onions, chopped
- ½ green bell pepper, chopped
- 4 garlic cloves, minced
- 1 oz fresh dill, divided, chopped
- 5 cups low-sodium chicken broth
- 1 lb gold potatoes, thinly sliced into rounds (best to use a mandolin slicer)
- 1 carrot, thinly sliced into rounds (best to use a mandolin slicer)
- 1 tsp dry oregano
- ¾ tsp ground coriander
- ½ tsp ground cumin
- Kosher salt and black pepper
- 1 lb salmon fillet, no skin, cut into large chunks
- Zest and juice of 1 lemon

Preparation

1. Heat 2 tablespoon extra virgin olive oil in a large pot until shimmering but not smoking. Add green onions, bell pepper, and garlic and cook over medium-heat, stirring frequently until fragrant (about 3 minutes or so). Add ½ of the fresh dill, and stir for 30 seconds more.
2. Now add broth, potatoes and carrots. Add spices and season with kosher salt and black pepper. Bring to a rolling boil then lower heat to medium and cook for 5 to 6 minutes or until the potatoes and carrots are tender.
3. Season salmon with kosher salt and gently add it to the pot of simmering soup. Lower heat and cook for a few brief minutes until salmon is cooked through about 3 to 5 minutes or until salmon is cooked and flakes easily.
4. Stir in lemon zest, lemon juice and remaining dill.
5. Transfer salmon soup to serving bowls. Serve with a side of your favorite crusty bread. Enjoy!

Easy Authentic Falafel Recipe: Step-By-Step

Prep Time: 30 minutes
Cook Time: 20 minutes
Servings 4

Ingredients

- 2 cups dried chickpeas (Do NOT use canned or cooked chickpeas)
- ½ tsp baking soda
- 1 cup fresh parsley leaves, stems removed
- ¾ cup fresh cilantro leaves, stems removed
- ½ cup fresh dill, stems removed
- 1 small onion, quartered
- 7-8 garlic cloves, peeled
- Salt to taste
- 1 tbsp ground black pepper
- 1 tbsp ground cumin
- 1 tbsp ground coriander
- 1 tsp cayenne pepper, optional
- 1 tsp baking powder
- 2 tbsp toasted sesame seeds
- Oil for frying

Falafel Sauce
- Tahini Sauce

Fixings for falafel sandwich (optional)
- Pita pockets
- English cucumbers, chopped or diced
- Tomatoes, chopped or diced
- Baby Arugula
- Pickles

Preparation

1. (One day in advance) Place the dried chickpeas and baking soda in a large bowl filled with water to cover the chickpeas by at least 2 inches. Soak overnight for 18 hours (longer if the chickpeas are still too hard). When ready, drain the chickpeas completely and pat them dry.
2. Add the chickpeas, herbs, onions, garlic and spices to the large bowl of a food processor fitted with a blade. Run the food processor 40 seconds at a time until all is well combined forming a the falafel mixture.
3. Transfer the falafel mixture to a container and cover tightly. Refrigerate for at least 1 hour or (up to one whole night) until ready to cook.
4. Just before frying, add the baking powder and sesame seeds to the falafel mixture and stir with a spoon.
5. Scoop tablespoonfuls of the falafel mixture and form into patties (½ inch in thickness each). It helps to have wet hands as you form the patties.
6. Fill a medium saucepan 3 inches up with oil. Heat the oil on medium-high until it bubbles softly. Carefully drop the falafel patties in the oil, let them fry for about 3 to 5 minutes or so until crispy and medium brown on the outside. Avoid crowding the falafel in the saucepan, fry them in batches if necessary.
7. Place the fried falafel patties in a colander or plate lined with paper towels to drain.
8. Serve falafel hot next to other small plates; or assemble the falafel patties in pita bread with tahini or hummus, arugula, tomato and cucumbers. Enjoy!

Easy Roasted Tomato Basil Soup (Vegan, GF)

Prep Time: 10 minutes
Cook Time: 50 minutes
Servings 6

Ingredients

- 3 lb Roma tomatoes halved
- 2 to 3 carrots peeled and cut into small chunks
- Extra virgin olive oil (I used Private Reserve Greek EVOO)
- Salt and pepper
- 2 medium yellow onions chopped
- 5 garlic cloves minced
- 1 cup canned crushed tomatoes
- 2 oz fresh basil leaves
- 3 to 4 fresh thyme sprigs
- 2 teaspoon thyme leaves
- 1 teaspoon dry oregano
- ½ teaspoon paprika
- ½ teaspoon ground cumin
- 2 ½ cups water
- Splash of lime juice optional

Preparation

1. Heat oven to 450 degrees F.
2. In a large mixing bowl, combine tomatoes and carrot pieces. Add a generous drizzle of extra virgin olive oil, and season with kosher salt and black pepper. Toss to combine.
3. Transfer to a large baking sheet and spread well in one layer. Roast in heated oven for about 30 minutes. When ready, remove from the heat and set aside for about 10 minutes to cool.
4. Transfer the roasted tomatoes and carrots to the large bowl of a food processor fitted with a blade. Add just a tiny bit of water and blend.
5. In a large cooking pot, heat 2 tablespoon extra virgin olive oil over medium-high heat until shimmering but not smoking. Add onions and cook for about 3 minutes, then add garlic and cook briefly until golden.
6. Pour the roasted tomato mixture into the cooking pot. Stir in crushed tomatoes, 2 ½ cups water, basil, thyme and spices. Season with a little kosher salt and black pepper. Bring to a boil, then lower heat and cover part-way. Let simmer for about 20 minutes or so.
7. Remove the thyme springs and transfer tomato basil soup to serving bowls. If you like, add a splash of lime juice and a generous drizzle of extra

Nutrition Fact

Calories: 104.9kcal Carbohydrates: 23.4g Protein: 4.3g Fat: 0.8g Saturated Fat: 0.1g Sodium: 93.6mg Potassium: 889.9mg Fiber: 5.4g Sugar: 14.3g Vitamin A: 5965.7IU Vitamin C: 43.8mg Calcium: 92mg Iron: 2mg

Black Eyed Peas Recipe (Greek Style)

Prep Time: 20 minutes
Cook Time: 30 minutes
Servings 4

Ingredients

- Extra virgin olive oil, I used Early Harvest Greek EVOO
- 1 large yellow onion, chopped
- 4 garlic cloves, chopped
- 1 green bell pepper, chopped
- 2 to 3 carrots, peeled and chopped
- 1 15- oz can diced tomato
- 2 cups water
- 1 dry bay leaf
- 1 ½ teaspoon ground cumin
- 1 teaspoon dry oregano
- ½ teaspoon paprika
- Kosher salt and black pepper
- ½ teaspoon red pepper flakes, optional
- 2 15- oz cans black eyed peas, drained and rinsed
- 1 lime or lemon, juice of
- 1 cup chopped fresh parsley

Preparation

1. In a large pot or Dutch oven, heat extra virgin olive oil over medium heat till shimmering but not smoking. Add onions and garlic. Sauté briefly until translucent and fragrant. Add bell peppers and carrots. Cook for 5 minutes, tossing regularly.
2. Now add diced tomatoes (with their juices), water, bay leaf, spices, salt and pepper. Raise the heat and bring to a boil. Add in the black-eyed peas. Boil for 5 minutes, then lower heat. Cover part-way and let simmer for 25 to 30 minutes (occasionally check to stir. If the black-eyed pea stew looks too dry, add a tiny bit of water.)
3. Finally, stir in lemon juice and parsley.
4. To serve, transfer to bowls. Add a generous drizzle of extra virgin olive oil. Enjoy with a side of warm Greek pita or on top of orzo, rice, or your favorite grain.

Nutrition Fact

Calories: 210.6kcal Carbohydrates: 40.1g Protein: 12.8g Fat: 1.2g Saturated Fat: 0.3g Polyunsaturated Fat: 0.5g Monounsaturated Fat: 0.2g Sodium: 239.9mg Potassium: 757.8mg Fiber: 12.2g Sugar: 9g Vitamin A: 4573.1IU Vitamin C: 43.3mg Calcium: 104.9mg Iron: 5.7mg

Juicy Mediterranean-Style Salmon Burgers

Prep Time: 15 minutes
Cook Time: 4 minutes
Servings 4

Ingredients

- 1 ½ lb skinless salmon fillet, cut into chunks
- 2 teaspoon Dijon mustard
- 2-3 tablespoon minced green onions
- 1 cup chopped fresh parsley
- 1 teaspoon ground coriander
- 1 teaspoon ground sumac
- ½ teaspoon sweet paprika
- ½ teaspoon black pepper
- Kosher Salt
- Italian breadcrumbs for coating, about ⅓ cup or so
- ¼ cup extra virgin olive oil

Salmon Burger Toppings

- Tzatziki Sauce, find the recipe here
- 6 oz baby arugula more to your liking
- 1 red onion, sliced

To Serve

- Bread of of your choice, optional, I often use whole wheat buns or Italian ciabatta rolls

Preparation

1. Place about ¼ of the salmon in the bowl of a large food processor. Add mustard. Run processor until the mixture is pasty. Transfer to a bowl.
2. Place the rest of the salmon in the food processor, and pulse just a couple times until coarsely chopped into ¼-inch pieces (do not over process this second batch of salmon, it should not get too fine or pasty, it should still have some texture.) Transfer to the same bowl.
3. Now add the minced green onions, parsley, and spices (coriander, sumac, paprika, black pepper). Season with kosher salt. Mix well until the mixture is combined. Cover and chill in the fridge for about ½ hour.
4. While the salmon chills, prepare the toppings. Make the Greek Tzatziki Sauce according to this recipe
5. Prepare the arugula, sliced tomatoes, and the remaining toppings and buns to serve.
6. When ready, take salmon mixture out of the fridge. Divide into 4 equal parts. Form into 1-inch think patties.
7. Place bread crumbs on a plate. Place each patty in the breadcrumbs plate and press to coat on one side, turn over and press on the other side to coat. Place the breaded salmon patties on a sheet pan lined with parchment paper.
8. Cook salmon patties. Heat about 3 tablespoon extra virgin olive oil over medium-high heat until shimmering but not smoking. Lower each of the patties carefully and cook, for 2 to 4 minutes, turning over once, until lightly browned on both sides and medium-rare within), (adjust heat as necessary during cooking to keep things sizzling and cooking well but without scorching the bread crumbs.) (minimum internal temp should be 115 to 120°F on an instant-read thermometer for medium-rare.)
9. Set cooked salmon burgers onto paper towel to drain any excess oil; sprinkle lightly with Kosher salt if you like. Add a squeeze of fresh lemon juice on top.
10. Assemble in prepared buns. Spread the buns with a bit of tzatziki sauce. Add the salmon, then layer on the arugula, tomato and onion slices…enjoy!

Creamy Tahini Date Banana Shake

Prep Time: 5 minutes
Cook Time: 0 minutes
Servings 3

INGREDIENTS

- 2 frozen bananas, sliced
- 4 pitted Medjool dates (if they're too big, you can chop them up a bit.)
- ¼ cup tahini (I used Soom tahini)
- ¼ cup crushed ice
- 1 ½ cups unsweetened almond milk
- Pinch ground cinnamon, more for later

Preparation

1. Place the sliced frozen bananas in your blender, add the remaining Ingredients. Run blender until you achieve a smooth and creamy shake.
2. Transfer the banana date shakes to serving cups and add pinch more ground cinnamon on top. Enjoy!

Simple Green Juice Recipe + Tips

Prep Time: 15 minutes
Cook Time: 0 minutes
Servings 2

Ingredients

- 1 bunch kale (about 5 oz)
- 1 inch piece fresh ginger, peeled
- 1 Granny smith apple (or any large apple)
- 5 celery stalks, ends trimmed
- ½ large English cucumber
- Handful fresh parsley (about 1 oz)

Preparation

1. Wash and prep the vegetables. I like to cut them in large chunks.
2. Juice in the order listed (or add them to a blender and blend on high.)
3. If you used a juicer, simply pour the green juice into glasses and enjoy immediately. If you used a blender, the juice will be thicker. You can pour it through a fine mesh sieve, and using the back of a spoon, press the pulp into the sieve to extract as much liquid as possible. Pour the strained juice into glasses and enjoy!

Mediterranean Baked Fish Recipe with Tomatoes And Capers

Prep Time: 5 minutes
Cook Time: 30 minutes
Servings 6

Ingredients

- ⅓ cup Private Reserve Greek extra virgin olive oil
- 1 small red onion, finely chopped
- 2 large tomatoes, diced (3 cups diced tomatoes. Use quality canned tomatoes, if you like)
- 10 garlic cloves, chopped
- 1 ½ tsp organic ground coriander
- 1 tsp all-natural sweet Spanish paprika
- 1 tsp organic ground cumin
- ½ tsp cayenne pepper (optional)
- 1 ½ tbsp capers
- Salt and pepper
- ⅓ cup golden raisins
- 1 ½ lb white fish fillet such as cod fillet or halibut fillet (wild, if possible)
- Juice of ½ lemon or more to your liking
- Zest of 1 lemon
- Fresh parsley or mint for garnish

Preparation

1. Prepare the tomato and capers sauce. In a medium saucepan, heat extra virgin olive oil over medium-high heat until shimmering but not smoking. Add onions, cook for 3 minutes until it begins to turn gold in color, tossing regularly. Add tomatoes, garlic, spices, pinch of salt (not too much) and pepper, capers, and raisins. Bring to a boil, then turn heat down to medium-low and let simmer for 15 minutes or so.
2. Heat oven to 400 degrees F.
3. Pat fish dry and season with salt and pepper on both sides.
4. Pour ½ of the cooked tomato sauce into the bottom of a 9 ½" x 13" baking dish. Arrange the fish on top. Add lemon juice and lemon zest, then top with the remaining tomato sauce.
5. Bake in 400 degrees F heated-oven for 15 to 18 minutes or until fish is cooked through and flakes easily (do not over-cook). Remove from heat and garnish with fresh parsley or mint to your liking.
6. Serve hot with Mediterranean grilled zucchini, Greek potatoes, or Lebanese rice. (See other suggestions for sides or salads up in the post)

Easy Mediterranean baked fish recipe with tomatoes and capers. A bright, delicate and flavor-packed baked fish that comes together in just 35 minutes! Make your salads and sides before you make the fish.

Nutrition Facts

Calories 308 % Daily Value* Total Fat 17.4g 22% Sodium 146.9mg 6% Total Carbohydrate 13.3g 5% Dietary Fiber 2g 7% Sugars 7.8g Protein 27g 54% Vitamin A12%Vitamin C18%Calcium3%Iron7%Vitamin D160%Magnesium12%Potassium16%Zinc7%Phosphorus27%Thiamin (B1)17%Riboflavin (B2)22%Niacin (B3)65%Vitamin B660%Folic Acid (B9)6%Vitamin B12222%Vitamin E11%Vitamin K15%

Greek Chicken and Potatoes

Prep Time: 20 minutes
Cook Time: 45 minutes
Servings 6

Ingredients

For Chicken and Potatoes
- 3 lb chicken pieces, bone in and skin on (I used 2 breasts and 3 legs)
- Salt
- 4 gold potatoes (about 2 lb), scrubbed clean, cut into thin wedges
- 1 medium yellow onion, halved, sliced
- 1 tsp black pepper
- 1 lemon, sliced
- 1 cup chicken broth
- 6 to 12 pitted quality kalamata olives
- Fresh parsley, for garnish

For the Lemon-Garlic Sauce (can also be used as marinade)
- ¼ cup extra virgin olive oil (I used Private Reserve Greek extra virgin olive oil)
- ¼ cup lemon juice
- 12 fresh garlic cloves, minced
- 1 ½ tbsp dried rosemary (or dried oregano)
- ½ tsp ground nutmeg

Sides (optional)
- Greek Salad
- Tzatziki Sauce
- Pita Bread

Preparation

1. Preheat oven to 350 degrees F.
2. Pat chicken dry and season generously with salt (lift the skins and apply salt underneath as well). (see optional step in notes)
3. Arrange potato wedges and onions in the bottom of a baking dish or pan. Season with salt and 1 teaspoon black pepper. Add the chicken pieces (see optional step in notes).
4. Make the lemon-garlic sauce. In a small mixing bowl, whisk together ¼ cup extra virgin olive oil with lemon juice, minced garlic, rosemary, and nutmeg. Pour evenly over the chicken and potatoes.
5. Arrange lemon slices on top. Pour chicken broth into the pan from one side (do not pour broth over the chicken).
6. Bake in heated oven uncovered for 45 minutes to 1 hour, until chicken and potatoes are tender. (Chicken's internal temperature should register at 165 degrees F). If you like, place the pan under the broiler briefly to allow the chicken skins to gain more color (watch carefully).
7. Remove from heat and add kalamata olives, if you like. Garnish with a little bit of fresh parsley.
8. Serve with Greek salad Taztaziki sauce and a side of pita bread, if you like. Enjoy!

This easy Greek chicken and potatoes recipe is a family favorite. The secret is in the lemon-garlic sauce, which doubles up as a marinade. Whether you choose to marinate the chicken for a couple of hours (I usually don't) or cook it right away, the flavors will surprise you in the best way possible.

Nutrition Facts

Calories 473 % Daily Value* Total Fat 15.8g 20% Saturated Fat 2.8g Trans Fat 0g Total Carbohydrate 28g 10% Dietary Fiber 3.5g 13% Sugars 3.1g Protein 54.4g 109% Vitamin A3%Vitamin C52%Calcium5%Iron13%Magnesium24%Potassium29%Zinc19%Phosphorus46%Thiamin (B1)29%Riboflavin (B2)36%Niacin (B3)146%Vitamin B6136%Folic Acid (B9)14%

Mediterranean-Style Sautéed Shrimp and Zucchini

Prep Time: 10 minutes
Cook Time: 12 minutes
Servings 4

Ingredients

For Chicken and Potatoes
- 1 ½ tablespoon dry oregano
- 1 teaspoon ground cumin
- 1 teaspoon ground coriander
- ½ teaspoon sweet paprika
- 1 lb large shrimp prawns, peeled, and deveined
- 2 tablespoon Extra virgin olive oil I used Private Reserve Greek EVOO
- ½ medium red onion thinly sliced
- 5 garlic cloves minced and divided
- 1 bell pepper cored and sliced into sticks
- 1 to 2 zucchini halved length-wise, sliced into ½ moons (you can use 1 zucchini and 1 yellow squash)
- 1 cup cooked chickpeas from canned chickpeas, drained
- 1 ½ cups cherry tomatoes halved
- Pinch kosher salt
- Pinch black pepper
- 1 large lemon juice of
- Handful fresh basil leaves torn or sliced into ribbons (you can use a different herb, depending on what's available to you)

Preparation

1. In a small bowl, combine the spices (oregano, cumin, coriander, and paprika.)
2. Pat shrimp dry and season with kosher salt and 1 ½ teaspoon of the spice mixture. Set aside briefly or refrigerate till later. (Reserve the remaining spice mixture for the vegetables.)
3. In a large cast iron skillet, heat 2 tablespoon extra virgin olive oil over medium heat. Add onions and ½ the amount of garlic and cook for 3 to 4 minutes, tossing regularly till fragrant (do not allow the garlic to burn.)
4. Add zucchini, bell peppers, and chickpeas. Season with salt and pepper and the remaining spice mixture. Toss to combine. If needed, raise the heat just a bit and cook the veggies until tender, tossing regularly (about 5 to 7 minutes.)
5. Transfer the veggies to a large plate for now. Return the skillet to the heat and add a little bit of extra virgin olive oil. Add the seasoned shrimp and remaining garlic. Cook over medium-high heat, stirring occasionally, until shrimp is totally pink (about 4 to 5 minutes).
6. Add the cooked vegetables back to the skillet with the shrimp. Add cherry tomatoes and lemon juice. Give everything a good toss. Finish with the fresh basil.

Nutrition Fact

Calories: 298.7kcal Carbohydrates: 23.9g Protein: 29.3g Fat: 10.4g Saturated Fat: 1.4g Polyunsaturated Fat: 2.2g Monounsaturated Fat: 5.6g Cholesterol: 285.8mg Sodium: 455mg Potassium: 642.9mg Fiber: 6.9g Sugar: 7.2g Vitamin A: 1483.1IU Vitamin C: 81.4mg Calcium: 257.6mg Iron: 5.8mg

Mediterranean Salmon Kabobs

Prep Time: 10 minutes
Cook Time: 8 minutes
Servings 5-6

Ingredients

For Marinade

- ¼ cup to ⅓ cup Extra Virgin Olive Oil (I used Early Harvest Greek olive oil)
- 1 lemon, zested and juiced
- 3 garlic cloves, minced
- 2 tsp chopped fresh thyme leaves
- 2 tsp dry oregano
- 1 tsp ground cumin
- 1 tsp mild chili pepper (I used this Aleppo pepper)
- ½ tsp ground coriander

- 1.5 lb Salmon fillet, cut into cubes approximately 1-inch to 1-½ inch or so in size
- 1 zucchini, sliced into rounds
- 1 small red onion, cut into squares
- Kosher salt and pepper

Preparation

1. In a small bowl, whisk together the marinade Ingredients of extra virgin olive oil, lemon juice and zest, garlic, oregano, thyme, cumin, Aleppo pepper and coriander.
2. Place salmon pieces, zucchini and onions in a large mixing bowl. Season with kosher salt and pepper, and toss briefly. Now pour the marinade over the salmon and toss again to make sure the salmon is well coated with the marinade. Let the fish marinate for about 15 to 20 minutes (see Cook's Tip)
3. Beginning with salmon, thread salmon, zucchini and onions through skewers (if using wooden skewers, be sure to have soaked them for 30 minutes before using.)
4. Heat an outdoor grill (indoor grilling instructions in notes). Arrange salmon skewers on top and cover the grill. Grill salmon kabobs for 6 to 8 minute, covered, or until the fish is opaque throughout, turning once midway through cooking (using tongs is the best way to turn the salmon skewers)

Best grilled salmon kabobs, prepared Mediterranean-style with a garlicy, zesty marinade, zucchini and onions! Serve these with your favorite Mediterranean salads and sides and a little Tahini sauce or Tzatziki (lots of ideas up in the post).

Nutrition Facts

Calories 295 % Daily Value* Total Fat 15.6g 20% Saturated Fat 3.7g   Trans Fat 0g Sodium 292.5mg 13% Total Carbohydrate 15.4g 6% Sugars 7.5g Protein 25.1g 50% Vitamin C6%Calcium3%Iron2%Magnesium9%Potassium2%Zinc1 Phosphorus1%Thiamin (B1)2%Riboflavin (B2)1%Vitamin B63%Folic Acid (B9)2%Vitamin K1%

Greek Shrimp with Tomatoes and Feta (Shrimp Saganaki)

Prep Time: 10 minutes
Cook Time: 20 minutes
Servings 6

Ingredients

For Marinade

- ½ pounds jumbo shrimp, 21/25, fully thawed, peeled and deveined
- Kosher salt
- 1 ½ teaspoons dry oregano, divided
- 1 ½ teaspoons dry dill weed, divided
- Pinch red pepper flakes
- 6 garlic cloves, minced, divided
- Extra virgin olive oil, I used Early Harvest Greek EVOO
- Black pepper
- 1 large red onion, chopped
- 1 26- ounce can diced tomato, drain only some of the liquid
- Juice of ½ lemon, more for later if you like
- Chopped fresh mint leaves, a generous handful
- Chopped fresh parsley leaves, a generous handful
- 2 ounces Greek feta cheese, more if you like
- 6 pitted Kalamata olives, chopped (optional)

Preparation

1. Pat shrimp dry and place in a large bowl. Season with kosher salt, pepper, ½ teaspoon dry oregano, ½ teaspoon dry dill weed, pinch red pepper flakes, and about ½ teaspoon of minced garlic. Drizzle with extra virgin olive oil, and toss to combine. Set aside for now.
2. In a large heavy skillet (I used this cast iron skillet), heat about 2 tablespoon extra virgin olive oil over medium heat until shimmering but not smoking. Add the chopped onion and remaining minced garlic, cook briefly until fragrant (stir regularly.) Add tomatoes and lemon juice, and season with pinch of salt, pepper, and remaining dry oregano and dill. Bring to a boil, then lower heat to medium-low and let simmer for 15 minutes.
3. Add the marinated shrimp. Cook for 5 to 7 minutes or until pink; do a little stirring if needed. (Do not overcook shrimp.)
4. Stir in fresh mint and parsley leaves. Finish with a sprinkle of feta and Kalamata olives. If you like, add a splash of lemon juice or more red pepper flakes to your taste.
5. Serve over plain orzo, your favorite grain, or your favorite crusty bread to sop upthe delicious sauce. Enjoy!

Easy Greek shrimp recipe (shrimp saganaki) cooked in flavor-packed tomato sauce and finished with fresh herbs, feta cheese, and olives. While it only takes 30 minutes to make, it is so elegant that it will wow your tastebuds (and your friends!). Serve shrimp saganaki with orzo, your favorite grain, or crusty bread to sop up all the delicious sauce.

Nutrition Fact

Calories: 146kcal Carbohydrates: 9.7g Protein: 18.3g Fat: 4g Saturated Fat: 1.5g Polyunsaturated Fat: 0.3g Monounsaturated Fat: 1g Trans Fat: 0.01g Cholesterol: 151.3mg Sodium: 989.5mg Potassium: 420mg Fiber: 2g Sugar: 3.8g Vitamin A: 427.2IU Vitamin C: 13.9mg Calcium: 170.1mg Iron: 1.9mg

Grilled Swordfish Recipe With A Mediterranean Twist

Prep Time: 15 minutes
Cook Time: 8 minutes
Servings 4

Ingredients

- 6 to 12 garlic cloves, peeled
- ⅓ cup extra virgin olive oil
- 2 tbsp fresh lemon juice, more for later
- 1 tsp coriander
- ¾ tsp cumin
- ½ to 1 teaspoon sweet Spanish paprika
- ¾ tsp salt
- ½ tsp freshly ground black pepper
- 4 swordfish steaks, about 5 to 6 ounces each, from sustainable sources
- Crushed red pepper, optional

Preparation

1. In a food processor, blend the garlic, lemon juice, olive oil, spices, salt and pepper for about three minutes or until well-combined forming a thick and smooth marinade.
2. Pat the swordfish steaks dry and place them in a pan (or a dish with sides to it) and apply the marinade generously on both sides and set aside for 15 minutes or so while you heat the grill.
3. Preheat a gas grill on high (be sure to oil the grates before using). When ready, grill the fish steaks on high heat for 5 to 6 minutes on one side, turn over once and grill on the other side for 3 minutes or so (the fish should flake easily, while maintain firmness. You will likely see a bit of pink on the inside, but it should cook through by the time it gets to the table).
4. Finish with a splash of fresh lemon juice and a sprinkle of crushed red pepper flakes if you like heat. Enjoy!

Easy grilled swordfish recipe that utilizes a delicious Mediterranean marinade with cumin, fresh garlic cloves and more. But you don't even need to leave it in the marinade too long! Just a few minutes while your grill is heating!

Nutrition Facts

Calories 398 % Daily Value* Total Fat 30.7g 39% Saturated Fat 5.3g   Trans Fat 0.1g Total Carbohydrate 3.1g 1% Dietary Fiber 0.6g 2% Sugars 0.4g Protein 28.4g57% Vitamin A8%Vitamin C6%Calcium2%Iron6%Vitamin D197%Magnesium11%Potassium14%Zinc10%Phosphorus30%Thiamin (B1)10%Riboflavin (B2)7%Niacin (B3)70%Vitamin B650%Folic Acid (B9)1%Vitamin B12100%Vitamin E21%Vitamin K5%

Greek Chicken Souvlaki Recipe with Tzatziki

Prep Time: 15 minutes
Cook Time: 8 minutes
Servings 4

Ingredients
For Souvlaki Marinade
- 10 garlic cloves, peeled
- 2 tbsp dried oregano
- 1 tsp dried rosemary
- 1 tsp sweet paprika
- 1 tsp each Kosher salt and black pepper
- ¼ cup extra virgin olive oil
- ¼ cup dry white wine
- Juice of 1 lemon
- 2 bay leaves

Pita Fixings
- Greek pita bread
- Tzatziki Sauce (make according to this recipe)
- Sliced tomato, cucumber, onions, and Kalamata olives

For Chicken
2 ½ lb organic boneless skinless chicken breast, fat removed, cut into 1 ½ inch pieces

Preparation
1. Prepare the marinade. In the bowl of a small food processor, add garlic, oregano, rosemary, paprika, salt, pepper, olive oil, white wine, and lemon juice (do NOT add the dried bay leaves yet). Pulse until well combined.
2. Place chicken in a large bowl and add bay leaves. Top with marinade. Toss to combine, making sure chicken is well-coated with marinade. Cover tightly and refrigerate for 2 hours or overnight (see note for quicker marinating option.)
3. Soak 10 to 12 wooden skewers in water for 30 to 45 minutes or so. Prepare Tzatziki sauce and other fixings, and if you're adding Greek salad or other sides, prepare those as well. (some sides like roasted garlic hummus may take longer, you can prepare those in advance).
4. When ready, thread marinated chicken pieces through the prepared skewers.
5. Prepare outdoor grill (or griddle). Brush grates with a little oil and heat over medium-high heat. T. Place chicken skewers on grill (or cook in batches on griddle) until well browned and internal temperature registers 155° on instant read thermometer. Be sure to turn skewers evenly to cook on all sides, about 5 minutes total. While grilling, brush lightly with the marinad.
6. Transfer chicken to serving platter and let rest for 3 minutes. Meanwhile, briefly grill pitas and keep warm.
7. Assemble grilled chicken souvlaki pitas. First, spread Tzatziki sauce on pita, add chicken pieces (take them off skewers first, of course) then add veggies and olives.
8. Optional: if you want more items to add to your buffet, consider Greek salad, watermelon salad, roasted garlic hummus, or a big Mezze platter.

All-star chicken souvlaki recipe takes you to the streets of Athens. Best souvlaki marinade; instructions for indoor/outdoor grilling & what to serve along.

Nutrition Fact
Calories 168 % Daily Value* Total Fat 7.7g 10% Saturated Fat 1.5g Trans Fat 0g Sodium 273.5mg 12% Total Carbohydrate 1.8g 1% Sugars 0.2g Protein 22g 44% Vitamin A2%Vitamin C3%Calcium3%Iron4%Magnesium7%Potassium7%Zinc7%Phosphorus17%Thiamin (B1)

Sicilian-Style Fish Stew

Recipe

Prep Time: 10 minutes
Cook Time: 35 minutes
Servings 4-6

Ingredients

- Private Reserve extra virgin olive oil
- 1 large yellow onion, chopped
- 2 celery ribs, chopped
- Salt and pepper
- 4 large garlic cloves, minced
- ½ tsp dried thyme
- Pinch red pepper flakes
- ¾ cup dry white wine
- 1 28-oz can whole peeled plum tomatoes, juice separated and reserved
- 3 cups low-sodium vegetable broth
- ¼ cup golden raisins
- 2 tbsp capers, rinsed
- 2 lb skinless sea bass fillet, about 1 ½-inch thick, cut into large cubes
- ½ cup chopped fresh parsley leaves, stems removed
- 3 tbsp toasted pine nuts, optional
- Crusty Italian bread for serving

Preparation

1. Heat 1 tablespoon olive oil in 5-quart Dutch oven (like this one) over medium heat. Add onions, celery, and a little salt and pepper (about ½ teaspoon each). Cook, stirring regularly, until softened (about 4 minutes). Add thyme, red pepper flakes and garlic and cook briefly until fragrant (about 30 more seconds).
2. Now, stir in the white wine and reserved tomato juice from can. Bring to a simmer, and cook until the liquid is reduced by about ½. Add the tomatoes, vegetable broth, raisins, and capers. Cook for 15-20 minutes over medium heat until flavors combine.
3. Pat the fish dry and season lightly with salt and pepper. Insert the fish pieces into the cooking liquid, and give everything a gentle stir so that the fish pieces are nicely covered in the cooking liquid. Bring to a simmer and cook for another 5 minutes. Remove the Dutch oven from the heat and cover. Let sit off heat for another 4-5 minutes so that the fish will finish cooking. Fish should be flaky when gently pulled apart with a paring knife. Finally, stir in the chopped parsley.
4. Ladle the hot fish stew into serving bowls, top each with a few toasted pine nuts, if you like. Serve with your favorite crusty bread! Enjoy!

An all-star recipe for fish stew with a Sicilian twist! The comfort of Italian flavors in one delicious stew cooked in a white wine-tomato broth with garlic, capers, raisins more!

Nutrition Facts

Calories 320 % Daily Value* Total Fat 11.6g 15% Saturated Fat 2.1g Trans Fat 0g Sodium 801.6mg 35% Total Carbohydrate 19.8g 7% Sugars 10g Protein 31.2g 62% Vitamin A11%Vitamin C16%Calcium6%Iron16%Vitamin D85%Magnesium26%Potassium18%Zinc13%Phosphorus28%Thiamin (B1)32%Riboflavin (B2)23%Niacin (B3)25%Vitamin B643%Folic Acid (B9)7%Vitamin B1219%Vitamin E17%Vitamin K10%

Italian-Style Sheet Pan Chicken With Vegetables

Prep Time: 10 minutes
Cook Time: 20 minutes
Servings 5

Ingredients

- 2 medium zucchini about 11 oz, halved length-wise then sliced into half moons
- 1 large red pepper cored, cut into chunks
- 1 red onion cut into chunks
- 9 oz baby broccoli trimmed and cut into pieces of equal size
- 1 ½ lb boneless chicken breast cut into bite-size pieces
- 5 garlic cloves minced
- Kosher salt and black pepper
- 2 teaspoon Dry oregano
- 1 teaspoon Paprika
- 1 teaspoon coriander
- 1 lemon zested and juiced
- 1 teaspoon white vinegar
- Extra virgin olive oil I used Private Reserve Greek EVOO
- Fresh parsley for garnish optional

Preparation

1. Heat the oven to 400 degrees F.
2. Place the cut veggies in a large mixing bowl. Add chicken pieces and minced garlic. Season with kosher salt and black pepper. Add spices. Now add lemon zest, lemon juice, vinegar, and a generous drizzle of extra virgin olive oil. Give everything a good toss to combine, making sure the veggies and chicken pieces are evenly coated.
3. Transfer the chicken and vegetables to a large sheet pan. Spread well in one layer.
4. Bake in heated oven for about 20 minutes until chicken is fully cooked through. If you want more color, place under the broiler briefly.
5. If you like, garnish with fresh parsley before serving (optional).

No fuss sheet pan chicken and vegetables, tossed with garlic, oregano, and a splash of citrus. A healthy weeknight meal & great for meal prep!

Nutrition Fact

Calories: 220.3kcal Carbohydrates: 13.4g Protein: 32.7g Fat: 4g Saturated Fat: 0.9g Cholesterol: 87.1mg Sodium: 415.2mg Potassium: 852.9mg Fiber: 3.4g Vitamin A: 2083.5IU Vitamin C: 107.6mg Calcium: 84.3mg Iron: 2mg

Mediterranean-Style Garlic Shrimp Recipe with Bell Peppers

Prep Time: 10 minutes
Cook Time: 15 minutes
Servings 4

Ingredients

- 1 ¼ lb large shrimp or prawns, peeled and deveined (if frozen, be sure to thaw first)
- 1 tablespoon all-purpose flour
- 1 to 2 teaspoon smoked Spanish paprika
- ½ teaspoon each salt and pepper
- ½ teaspoon ground coriander
- ¼ teaspoon cayenne
- ¼ teaspoon sugar
- 1 tablespoon butter I prefer to use ghee clarified butter
- 3 tablespoon Extra virgin olive oil
- ½ red onion, thinly sliced
- 4 garlic cloves, chopped
- ½ green bell pepper and ½ yellow bell pepper, cored and sliced
- 1 cup canned diced tomato
- ⅓ cup chicken or vegetable broth
- 2 tablespoon dry white wine
- 2 tablespoon fresh lemon juice
- ⅓ cup chopped parsley leaves

Preparation

1. Pat the shrimp dry and place it in a large bowl. Add the flour, smoked paprika, salt and pepper, coriander, cayenne, and sugar. Toss until the shrimp is well-coated.
2. In a large cast iron skillet, melt the butter with the olive oil over medium heat. Add the shallots and garlic. Cook for 2-3 minutes, stirring regularly, until fragrant (be sure not to burn the garlic.) Add the bell peppers and cook another 4 minutes or so, tossing occasionally.
3. Now add the shrimp. Cook for 1 to 2 minutes, then add the diced tomatoes, broth, white wine and lemon juice. Cook for a couple more minutes or until the shrimp turns bright orange.
4. Finally, stir in the chopped fresh parsley and serve!

Easy shrimp recipe, coated in Mediterranean spices and skillet-cooked in a light white wine and olive oil sauce with shallots, bell peppers and tomatoes. Ready in 25 minutes or less!

Nutrition Fact

Calories: 284.4kcal Carbohydrates: 9.9g Protein: 30.6g Saturated Fat: 1.8g Cholesterol: 357.6mg Sodium: 1258.1mg Potassium: 336mg Fiber: 1.8g Vitamin A: 155.1IU Vitamin C: 20mg Calcium: 247.7mg Iron: 4.2mg

Italian Baked Chicken Breast Recipe

Prep Time: 10 minutes
Cook Time: 18 minutes
Servings 6

Ingredients

- 2 lb boneless skinless chicken breast
- Salt and pepper
- 2 teaspoon dry oregano
- 1 teaspoon fresh thyme
- 1 teaspoon Sweet paprika
- 4 garlic cloves, minced
- 3 tablespoon Extra virgin olive oil
- Juice of ½ lemon
- 1 medium red onion, halved and thinly sliced
- 5 to 6 Campari tomatoes, or small Roma tomatoes, halved
- Handful chopped fresh parsley for garnish
- Fresh basil leaves for garnish

Preparation

1. Preheat oven to 425 degrees F.
2. Pat chicken dry. Place a chicken breast in a large zip-top bag and zip the top (make sure to release any air in the bag first), then place it on your poultry cutting board. Using a meat mallet like this one, pound to flatten the chicken. Repeat the process with the remaining chicken breast pieces.
3. Season the chicken with kosher salt and pepper on both sides and place in a large mixing bowl or dish. Add spices, minced garlic, extra virgin olive oil, and lemon juice. Combine to make sure the chicken is evenly coated with the spices and garlic.
4. In a large lightly oiled baking dish or pan, spread the onion slices on the bottom. Arrange seasoned chicken on top, and add the tomatoes.
5. Cover the baking dish tightly with foil and bake for 10 minutes covered, then uncover and bake for another 8 to 10 minutes or so. Watch carefully. This can take less or more time depending on the thickness of your chicken breasts. To be sure the chicken is cooked through, use an instant digital cooking thermometer. It should register 165 degrees F.
6. Remove from the heat. Let the chicken breasts rest (cover with foil or another pan) for 5 to 10 minutes or so before serving. Uncover and garnish with fresh parsley and basil. Enjoy!

Easy Italian baked chicken breast, flavored with a simple spice mixture along with fresh garlic and olive oil, and finished with parsley and fresh basil. Be sure to read the tips for best results.

Nutrition Fact

Calories: 191.8kcal Carbohydrates: 3.4g Protein: 32.6g Fat: 4.5g Saturated Fat: 1g Trans Fat: 0.1g Cholesterol: 96.8mg Sodium: 177.5mg Potassium: 641.6mg Fiber: 0.8g Vitamin A: 349.6IU Vitamin C: 6.3mg Calcium: 24.3mg Iron: 0.9mg

One-Pan Baked Halibut Recipe With Vegetables

Prep Time: 5 minutes
Cook Time: 15 minutes
Servings 6

Ingredients

For The Sauce:

- Zest of 2 lemons
- Juice of 2 lemons
- 1 cup extra virgin olive oil
- 1 ½ tablespoon freshly minced garlic
- 2 teaspoon dill weed
- 1 teaspoon seasoned salt, more for later
- ½ teaspoon ground black pepper
- 1 teaspoon dried oregano
- ½ to ¾ teaspoon ground coriander

For The Fish

- 1 pound fresh green beans
- 1 pound cherry tomatoes
- 1 large yellow onion, sliced into half moons
- 1 ½ pound halibut fillet, slice into 1 ½-inch pieces

Preparation

1. Preheat the oven to 425 degrees F.
2. In a large mixing bowl, whisk the sauce Ingredients together. Add the green beans, tomatoes, and onions and toss to coat with the sauce. With a large slotted spoon or spatula, transfer the vegetables to a large baking sheet (21 x 15 x 1 inch baking sheet, for example). Keep the vegetables to one side or one half of the baking sheet and make sure they are spread out in one layer.
3. Now, add the halibut fillet strips to the remaining sauce, toss to coat. Transfer the halibut fillet to the baking sheet next to the vegetables and pour any remaining sauce on top.
4. Lightly sprinkle the halibut and vegetables with a little more seasoned salt.
5. Bake in 425 degrees F heated oven for 15 minutes. Then transfer the baking sheet to the top oven rack and broil for another 3 minutes or so, watching carefully. The cherry tomatoes should begin to pop under the broiler.
6. When ready, remove the baked halibut and vegetables from the oven. Serve immediately.

You'll love this simple baked halibut recipe with colorful vegetables tossed in a citrus and olive oil sauce! Perfect for busy weeknights because it comes together in 20 minutes or less. If you can't find halibut, another white fish like cod, haddock, or red snapper would work well. This sheet pan dinner is a filling meal in one, but if you want to make the most of the zesty Mediterranean-style sauce, serve the halibut and veggies over a bed of barley or bulgur.

Nutrition Fact

Calories: 311.5kcal Carbohydrates: 11.1g Protein: 23.6g Fat: 19.8g Saturated Fat: 2.9g Polyunsaturated Fat: 2.4g Monounsaturated Fat: 13.7g Cholesterol: 55.6mg Sodium: 479.2mg Potassium: 861.4mg Fiber: 3.2g Sugar: 5.2g Vitamin A: 977IU Vitamin C: 28.5mg Calcium: 59.8mg Iron: 1.8mg

BEST Moroccan Fish Recipe

Prep Time: 10 minutes
Cook Time: 30 minutes
Servings 6

Ingredients

- Extra Virgin Olive Oil (I used Private Reserve EVOO)
- 8 garlic cloves, divided (4 minced cloves and 4 sliced)
- 2 tbsp tomato paste
- 2 medium tomatoes, diced
- 1 red pepper, cored, sliced
- 1 15-oz can chickpeas, drained &rinsed
- Large handful fresh cilantro
- 1 ½ cup water
- Kosher salt and black pepper
- 1 ½ tsp Ras El Hanout, divided
- 1 ½ lb cod fillet pieces (about ½ inch in thickness)
- ¾ tsp paprika
- ½ tsp cumin
- Juice of ½ lemon
- ½ lemon, sliced into thin rounds

Preparation

1. In a large pan with cover, heat 2 tablespoon extra virgin olive oil (I used Private Reserve) over medium heat until shimmering but not smoking.
2. Add minced garlic and cook very briefly, tossing regularly, until fragrant. Add tomato paste, diced tomato, and bell peppers. Cook for 3 to 4 minutes over medium heat, tossing frequently.
3. Now, add chickpeas, water, cilantro, and sliced garlic. Season with kosher salt and pepper. Stir in ½ teaspoon Ras El Hanout spice mixture. Raise heat, if needed, and bring to a boil. Lower heat. Cover part-way and let simmer for about 20 minutes. (Check occasionally and add a little water if needed.)
4. Meanwhile, in a small mixing bowl, combine remaining Ras El Hanout with cumin and paprika. Season the fish with kosher salt and pepper and the spice mixture on both sides. Add a generous drizzle of extra virgin olive oil. Work the fish to make sure it's well coated with the spices and the olive oil.
5. When ready, add the season fish to the pan, and make sure to nestle the fish pieces into the saucy chickpea and tomato mixture. Ladle a bit of the sauce on top of the fish. Add lemon juice and lemon slices. Cook another 10 to 15 minutes over medium-low until the fish is fully cooked and flaky. Garnish with more fresh cilantro.
6. Serve immediately with your favorite crusty bread, grain, or rice.

This delicious Moroccan fish recipe takes the fish dinner game to a new level of delicious! Braised cod recipe in a saucy chickpea, tomato, and bell pepper medley and lots of warm Moroccan flavors from Ras El Hanout, paprika and cumin.

Nutrition Fact

Calories 463 % Daily Value* Total Fat 5.7g 7% Saturated Fat 0.8g Trans Fat 0g   Monounsaturated Fat 1.8g   0% Sodium 135.5mg 6% Total Carbohydrate 67.2g 24% Sugars 5.1g Protein 23.7g 47% Vitamin A5%Vitamin C97%Calcium27%Iron28%Vitamin D1%Magnesium15%Potassium22%Zinc21%Phosphorus30%Thiamin (B1)34%Riboflavin (B2)19%Niacin (B3)13%Vitamin B6139%Folic Acid (B9)7%Vitamin B1224%Vitamin E7%Vitamin K9%

Baked Cod Recipe with Lemon And Garlic

Prep Time: 10 minutes
Cook Time: 22 minutes
Servings 5

Ingredients

- 1.5 lb Cod fillet pieces, 4-6 pieces
- ¼ cup chopped fresh parsley leaves

Lemon Sauce

- 5 tablespoon fresh lemon juice
- 5 tbsp extra virgin olive oil
- 2 tablespoon melted butter
- 5 garlic cloves, minced

For Coating

- ⅓ cup all-purpose flour
- 1 teaspoon ground coriander
- ¾ teaspoon sweet Spanish paprika
- ¾ teaspoon ground cumin
- ¾ teaspoon salt
- ½ teaspoon black pepper

Preparation Fact

1. Preheat oven to 400 degrees F.
2. Mix together the lemon juice, olive oil, and melted butter in a shallow bowl (do not add the garlic yet). Set aside.
3. In another shallow bowl, mix the all-purpose flour, spices, salt and pepper. Set next to the lemon sauce.
4. Pat the fish dry. Dip the fish in the lemon sauce then dip it in the flour mixture. Shake off excess flour. Reserve the lemon sauce for later.
5. Heat 2 tablespoon olive oil in a cast iron skillet (or an oven-safe pan) over medium-high heat (watch the oil to be sure it is shimmering but not smoking). Add the fish and sear on each side to give it some color, but do not fully cook (about 2 minutes on each side). Remove the skillet from heat.
6. To the remaining lemon sauce, add the minced garlic and mix. Drizzle all over the fish fillets.
7. Bake in the heated oven until the fish flakes easily with a fork (10 minutes should do it, but begin checking earlier). Remove from the heat and sprinkle chopped parsley. Serve immediately.

Best baked cod recipe out there! Prepared Mediterranean style with a few spices and a mixture of lemon juice, olive oil and lots of garlic. Bakes in 15 mins!

Nutrition Fact

Calories: 319.3kcal Carbohydrates: 9.6g Protein: 25.8g Fat: 19.8g Saturated Fat: 5g Trans Fat: 0.2g Cholesterol: 70.6mg Sodium: 466.1mg Potassium: 641.5mg Fiber: 1.2g Sugar: 0.5g Vitamin A: 603.3IU Vitamin C: 14.2mg Calcium: 45.3mg Iron: 1.7mg

Lebanese Rice With Vermicelli

Prep Time: 15 minutes
Cook Time: 20 minutes
Servings 6

Ingredients

- 2 cups long grain or medium grain rice
- Water
- 1 cup broken vermicelli pasta
- 2 ½ tbsp olive oil
- Salt
- ½ cup toasted pine nuts, optional to finish

Preparation

1. Rinse the rice well (a few times) then place it in a medium bowl and cover with water. Soak for 15 to 20 minutes. Test to see if you can easily break a grain of rice by simply placing it between your thumb and index finger. Drain well.
2. In a medium non-stick cooking pot, heat the olive oil on medium-high. Add the vermicelli and continuously stir to toast it evenly. Vermicelli should turn a nice golden brown, but watch carefully not to over-brown or burn it (If it burns, you must throw the vermicelli away and start over).
3. Add the rice and continue to stir so that the rice will be well-coated with the olive oil. Season with salt.
4. Now add 3 ½ cups of water and bring it to a boil until the water significantly reduces (see the photo below). Turn the heat to low and cover.
5. Cook for 15-20 minutes on low. Once fully cooked, turn the heat off and leave the rice undisturbed in it's cooking pot for 10-15 minutes, then uncover and fluff with a fork.
6. Transfer to a serving platter and top with the toasted pine nuts. Enjoy!

Vegan Lebanese rice with vermicelli and pine nuts. A great side dish next to many Mediterranean favorites.

Nutrition Fact

Calories 331 % Daily Value* Total Fat 5.4g 7% Sodium 0.9mg   0% Total Carbohydrate 61g   22% Sugars 0.4g Protein 6.4g 13% Iron3%Magnesium5%Potassium2%Zinc4%Phosphorus4%Thiamin (B1)5%Riboflavin (B2)3%Niacin (B3)8%Vitamin B62%Folic Acid (B9)3%

Simple Vegetarian Minestrone Soup

Prep Time: 10 minutes
Cook Time: 35 minutes
Servings 6

Ingredients

- ¼ cup extra virgin olive oil
- 1 small yellow onion, chopped
- 2 carrots, chopped
- 2 celery stalks, diced
- 4 garlic cloves, minced
- 1 zucchini or yellow squash, diced
- 1 cup green beans, fresh or frozen, trimmed and cut into 1-inch pieces, if needed
- Kosher salt and black pepper
- 1 teaspoon paprika
- ½ teaspoon rosemary
- 1 15-oz can crushed tomatoes
- 6 cups broth, vegetable or chicken broth
- 1-inch Parmesan cheese rind, optional
- 1 bay leaf
- 2 to 3 sprigs fresh thyme
- 1 (15-oz) can kidney beans
- Large handful chopped parsley
- Handful fresh basil leaves
- Grated Parmesan cheese, to serve (optional)
- 2 cups cooked ditalini or elbow pasta

Preparation

1. In a large Dutch oven, heat the extra virgin olive oil over medium heat until shimmering but not smoking. Add onions, carrots and celery. Raise heat to medium-high and cook stirring regularly, until the veggies soften a bit (about 5 minutes or so). Add the garlic and cook another minute, tossing regularly.
2. Add the zucchini or yellow squash and green beans. Season with paprika, rosemary, and a generous pinch of kosher salt and pepper. Toss to combine.
3. Now add the crushed tomatoes, broth, fresh thyme, bay leaf and Parmesan rind (if using.) Bring to a boil, then reduce the heat to a gentle simmer and partially cover the pot. Let simmer for about 20 minutes or so.
4. Uncover the pot and add the kidney beans. Cook for another 5 minutes.
5. Finally, Stir in the parsley and fresh basil. And, if serving immediately, stir in the cooked pasta and simmer just until the pasta is warmed through; do not overcook. (See Cook's Tip #2)
6. Remove the cheese rind and bay leaf. Taste and adjust seasoning to your liking. Serve the minestrone hot with a sprinkle of grated Parmesan and a drizzle of extra virgin olive oil.

Hearty vegetarian minestrone soup is an Italian speciality. Brimming with vegetables, kidney beans, and pasta, it's a great soup to use up what you have on hand. The thick, flavorful tomato broth is scented with rosemary, lots of fresh herbs, and Parmesan! One bowl will never be enough!

Nutrition Fact

Calories: 211.9kcal Carbohydrates: 26.7g Protein: 6.8g Saturated Fat: 1.5g Cholesterol: 0.7mg Potassium: 650.6mg Fiber: 7.4g Vitamin A: 4456.4IU Vitamin C: 19.4mg Calcium: 83.3mg Iron: 2.6mg

BEST Mediterranean Couscous Salad

Prep Time: 15 minutes
Cook Time: 10 minutes
Servings 6

Ingredients

- For the Lemon-Dill Vinaigrette
- 1 large lemon, juice of
- ⅓ cup extra virgin olive oil (I used Greek Private Reserve)
- 1 tsp dill weed
- 1 to 2 garlic cloves, minced
- Salt and pepper

For the Pearl Couscous

- 2 cups Pearl Couscous
- Private Reserve extra virgin olive oil
- 2 cups grape tomatoes, halved
- ⅓ cup finely chopped red onions
- ½ English cucumber, finely chopped
- 15 oz can chickpeas, drained and rinsed
- 14 oz can artichoke hearts, roughly chopped if needed
- ½ cup pitted kalamata olives
- 15-20 fresh basil leaves, roughly chopped or torn; more for garnish
- 3 oz fresh baby mozzarella (or feta cheese), optional

Preparation

1. To make the lemon-dill vinaigrette, place the vinaigrette Ingredients in a bowl. Whisk together to combine. Set aside briefly.
2. In a medium-sized heavy pot, heat two tablespoons of olive oil. Saute the couscous in the olive oil briefly until golden brown. Add 3 cups of boiling water (or the amount instructed on the package), and cook according to package. When ready, drain in a colander. Set aside in a bowl to cool.
3. In a large mixing bowl, combine the remaining Ingredients minus the basil and mozzarella. Then add the couscous and the basil and mix together gently.
4. Now, give the lemon-dill vinaigrette a quick whisk and add it to the couscous salad. Mix again to combine. Test and adjust salt, if needed.
5. Finally mix in the mozzarella cheese. Garnish with more fresh basil. Enjoy!

Mediterranean couscous salad recipe, loaded with nutrition and flavor from chickpeas, veggies, fresh herbs and a zippy lemon-dill vinaigrette. This versatile dish makes a great lunch, light supper, or side depending on what you need.   And you can make it ahead, the flavors deepen the next day. Be sure to watch my video and grab my tips in the post above.

Nutrition Fact

Calories 393 % Daily Value* Total Fat 13g 17% Saturated Fat 1.8g Trans Fat 0g   Total Carbohydrate 57.5g 21% Dietary Fiber 5.9g 21% Protein 13.1g 26% Vitamin A4%Vitamin C24%Calcium9%Iron10%Magnesium12%Potassium7%Zinc12%Phosphorus17%Thiamin (B1)13%Riboflavin (B2)8%Niacin (B3)15%Vitamin B610%Folic Acid (B9)19%Vitamin B123%Vitamin K15%

Simple Mushroom Barley Soup

Prep Time: 15 minutes
Cook Time: 30 minutes
Servings 4

Ingredients

- Extra virgin olive oil (I used Private Reserve Greek EVOO)
- 16 oz baby bella mushrooms, cleaned well and halved or sliced
- Kosher salt
- 1 yellow onion, chopped
- 4 garlic cloves, chopped
- 2 celery stalks, chopped
- 1 carrot, chopped
- 8 oz white mushrooms, cleaned and chopped
- ½ cup canned crushed tomatoes
- Black pepper
- 1 tsp coriander
- ½ tsp to ¾ teaspoon smoked paprika
- ½ tsp cumin
- 6 cups low-sodium broth (vegetable broth or beef broth)
- 1 cup pearl barley rinsed
- ½ cup packed chopped parsley

Preparation

1. In a large Dutch Oven, heat extra virgin olive oil over medium-high heat until shimmering but not smoking. Add baby bell mushrooms and cook until mushrooms soften and gain some color (about 5 minutes or so). Remove from the pot and set aside for now.
2. In the same pot, add a little more extra virgin olive oil. Add onions, garlic, celery, carrots, and chopped white mushrooms. Cook for 4 to 5 minutes over medium-high heat. Season with salt and pepper.
3. Now, add crushed tomatoes and spices (coriander, smoked paprika, cumin). Cook for 3 minutes or so, tossing regularly.
4. Add broth and pearl barley. Bring to a rolling boil for 5 minutes, then turn heat down. Cover and let simmer over low heat for about 30 minutes or until the barley is tender and cooked through.
5. Add the cooked bella mushrooms back to the pot and stir to combine. Cook for about 5 minutes or so until mushrooms are well warmed through.
6. Finish with fresh parsley. Transfer to serving bowls and enjoy!

Hearty mushrooms, chopped vegetables, and tender pearl barley make up this simple and satisfying mushroom barley soup. As comforting as your favorite deli's barley soup, but with even more flavor and a subtle smoky finish! Vegan and Mediterranean diet friendly.

Tuna Pasta Recipe, Mediterranean-Style

Prep Time: 10 minutes
Cook Time: 10 minutes
Servings 5

Ingredients

- ¾ lb spaghetti (or pasta of your choice)
- Kosher salt (I use Diamond Crystal)
- 1 ½ cups frozen peas
- Extra virgin olive oil (I use Private Reserve Greek extra virgin olive oil)
- 1 red bell pepper, cored and cut into thin strips
- 6 garlic cloves, minced
- 2 5- oz cans solid albicore tuna, drained
- Zest of 1 lemon
- Juice of ½ lemon, more to your liking
- Handful chopped fresh parsley (about 1 ounce)
- 1 teaspoon dried oregano
- Black pepper, to your liking
- 6 to 8 pitted kalmata olives sliced
- 1 jalapeno pepper (optional), sliced
- Grated Parmesan cheese to your liking

Preparation

1. Bring 3 quarts of water to a rolling boil and add 1 tablespoon of kosher salt. Cook the pasta in the boiling water to al dante according to package (most spaghetti will cook in 9 to 11 minutes or so). After the pasta has been cooking for 5 minutes, add the frozen peas to cook with the pasta for the remainder of the time. When the pasta is ready, take ¾ cup of the cooking water and set it aside. Drain the pasta and peas in a colander.
2. In a large, deep cooking pan, heat 2 tablespoon extra virgin olive oil over medium-high till shimmering but not smoking. Add the red bell peppers and cook for 3 to 4 minutes, tossing regularly. Add the garlic and cook, tossing frequently, for 30 seconds or so until fragrant.
3. Now, add the cooked pasta and peas to the pan and toss to combine. Add the tuna, lemon zest, lemon juice, parsley, oregano, black pepper, kalamata olives, jalapeno if using, and a big sprinkle of Parmesan cheese. Drizzle a bit of extra virgin olive oil and some of the pasta cooking water as needed. Give everything a toss. Taste and adjust seasoning to your liking.
4. Transfer the tuna pasta to serving bowls. Enjoy!

This darn delicious tuna pasta with peas comes together in 20 minutes. You'll love the bold flavors thanks to simple Ingredients like garlic, bell peppers, parsley, lemon zest, and a big sprinkle of Parmesan.

Nutrition Fact

Calories: 374.3kcal Carbohydrates: 58g Protein: 25.1g Saturated Fat: 0.7g Potassium: 456.9mg Fiber: 5.1g Vitamin A: 1119.5IU Vitamin C: 52.2mg Calcium: 42.8mg Iron: 2.3mg

How to Cook Couscous Perfectly Every Time!

Prep Time: 5 minutes
Cook Time: 10 minutes
Servings 5

Ingredients

- 1 cup low-sodium broth or water
- Extra virgin olive oil
- Kosher Salt
- 1 cup dry instant couscous I used this couscous
- To Flavor optional
- Pinch of cumin or spice of your choice
- 1 to 2 garlic clove minced and sauteed in extra virgin olive oil
- 2 green onions chopped
- Fresh herbs to your liking I used parsley and dill

Preparation

1. In a saucepan, add broth or water. Add a drizzle of extra virgin olive oil and a pinch of kosher salt. Bring to a boil.
2. Now, toast the couscous. In a non-stick skillet or pan, heat about 1 to 2 tablespoon extra virgin olive oil. Add the couscous and toss around with a wooden spoon until golden brown. This is an optional step but can really adds a great nutty flavor.
3. Stir couscous in the boiled liquid quickly and immediately turn the heat off. Cover and let sit for 10 minutes or until couscous has completely absorbed the broth or water.
4. Uncover and fluff with a fork.
5. You can serve couscous plain, or mix in spices and herbs to give it more flavor. If you like, add in a pinch of cumin, sautéed garlic, chopped green onions, and fresh herbs or your choice. Enjoy!

Learn how to cook couscous perfectly every time! It takes just 15 minutes and a handful of Ingredients. This quick couscous recipe is a great side next to your favorite protein, or use it as a bed to a tasty stew.

Nutrition Fact

Calories: 202kcal Carbohydrates: 34.2g Protein: 7.1g Fat: 1.1g Saturated Fat: 0.1g Sodium: 1.1mg Potassium: 16.6mg Fiber: 5.3g Vitamin A: 59.8IU Vitamin C: 1.4mg Calcium: 25mg Iron: 2mg

Mediterranean Roasted Vegetables Barley Recipe

Prep Time: 10 minutes
Cook Time: 40 minutes
Servings 6

Ingredients

- 1 cup/163 g dry pearl barley, washed
- Water
- 2 whole zucchini squash, diced
- 1 red bell pepper, cored, diced
- 1 yellow bell pepper, cored, diced
- 1 medium red onion, diced
- Salt and pepper
- 2 tsp/ 3.9 g harissa spice, divided
- ¾ tsp/ 1.95 g smoked paprika, divided
- Early Harvest Greek extra virgin olive oil
- 2 scallions (green onions), trimmed and chopped (both whites and greens)
- 1 garlic clove, minced
- 2 oz / 56 g chopped fresh parsley
- 2 tbsp/30 ml fresh squeezed lemon juice
- Feta cheese, to taste (optional)
- Toasted pine nuts, to taste (optional)

Preparation

1. Preheat oven to 425 degrees F.
2. Place pearl barley and 2 ½ cups water in a sauce pan. Bring to a boil, then turn heat down to low. Cover and cook anywhere from 30 to 45 minutes or until the barley is cooked through (should be tender but maintains some chew.)
3. While barley is cooking, place diced vegetables (zucchini, bell peppers, and red onion) on a large baking sheet. Season with salt, pepper, 1 ½ teaspoon harissa spice, and ½ teaspoon smoked paprika. Drizzle with extra virgin olive oil. Toss to coat. Spread evenly in one layer on the baking sheet. Roast in heated oven for 25 minutes or so.
4. When barley is ready, drain any excess water. Season with salt, pepper, ½ teaspoon harissa spice and ¼ teaspoon smoked paprika. Toss to combine.
5. Transfer cooked barley to a large mixing bowl. Add roasted veggies. Add chopped scallions, garlic, and fresh parsley. Dress with lemon juice and a good drizzle of Early Harvest extra virgin olive oil. Toss. If you like, top with crumbled feta and toasted pine nuts.
6. Serve warm, at room temperature, or cold! Enjoy.

Easy roasted vegetable barley recipe, prepared Mediterranean style with fresh herbs, spices, citrus and extra virgin olive oil.

Nutrition Fact

Calories 192 % Daily Value* Total Fat 5.4g 7% Sodium 206.2mg 9% Total Carbohydrate 33.2g   12% Sugars 3.9g Protein 4.6g 9% Vitamin A15%Vitamin C91%Calcium3%Iron10%Magnesium10%Potassium7%Zinc9%Phosphorus9%Thiamin (B1)10%Riboflavin (B2)8%Niacin (B3)14%Vitamin B617%Folic Acid (B9)13%Vitamin E6%Vitamin K206%

Easy Moroccan Vegetable Tagine Recipe

Prep Time: 15 minutes
Cook Time: 40 minutes
Servings 4-6

Ingredients

- ¼ cup Private Reserve extra virgin olive oil, more for later
- 2 medium yellow onions, peeled and chopped
- 8-10 garlic cloves, peeled and chopped
- 2 large carrots, peeled and chopped
- 2 large russet potatoes, peeled and cubed
- 1 large sweet potato, peeled and cubed
- Salt
- 1 tbsp Harissa spice blend
- 1 tsp ground coriander
- 1 tsp ground cinnamon
- ½ tsp ground turmeric
- 2 cups canned whole peeled tomatoes
- ½ cup heaping chopped dried apricot
- 1 quart low-sodium vegetable broth (or broth of your choice)
- 2 cups cooked chickpeas
- 1 lemon, juice of
- Handful fresh parsley leaves

Preparation

1. In a large heavy pot or Dutch Oven, heat olive oil over medium heat until just shimmering. Add onions and increase heat to medium-high. Saute for 5 minutes, tossing regularly.
2. Add garlic and all the chopped veggies. Season with salt and spices. Toss to combine.
3. Cook for 5 to 7 minutes on medium-high heat, mixing regularly with a wooden spoon.
4. Add tomatoes, apricot and broth. Season again with just a small dash of salt.
5. Keep the heat on medium-high, and cook for 10 minutes. Then reduce heat, cover and simmer for another 20 to 25 minutes or until veggies are tender.
6. Stir in chickpeas and cook another 5 minutes on low heat.
7. Stir in lemon juice and fresh parsley. Taste and adjust seasoning, adding more salt or harissa spice blend to your liking.
8. Transfer to serving bowls and top each with a generous drizzle of Private Reserve extra virgin olive oil. Serve hot with your favorite bread, couscous, or rice. Enjoy!

All-star vegetable tagine recipe! Simple vegetable stew packed with the perfect balance of Moroccan flavors. Vegan and Gluten free.

Nutrition Facts

Calories 448 % Daily Value* Total Fat 18.4g 24% Sodium 405.4mg 18% Total Carbohydrate 60.7g 22% Sugars 22.5g Protein 16.9g 34% Vitamin A62%Vitamin C36%Calcium17%Iron21%Magnesium17%Potassium31%Zinc14%Phosphorus23%Thiamin (B1)75%Riboflavin (B2)29%Niacin (B3)39%Vitamin B646%Folic Acid (B9)15%Vitamin B1218%Vitamin E12%Vitamin K18%

Sheet-Pan Chicken Thighs with Brussels Sprouts & Gnocchi

Prep Time: 20 minutes
Cook Time: 20 minutes
Servings 4

Ingredients

- 4 tablespoons extra-virgin olive oil, divided
- 2 tablespoons chopped fresh oregano, divided
- 2 large cloves garlic, minced, divided
- ½ teaspoon ground pepper, divided
- ¼ teaspoon salt, divided
- 1 pound Brussels sprouts, trimmed and quartered
- 1 (16 ounce) package shelf-stable gnocchi
- 1 cup sliced red onion
- 4 boneless, skinless chicken thighs, trimmed
- 1 cup halved cherry tomatoes
- 1 tablespoon red-wine vinegar

Preparation

Step 1: Preheat oven to 450 degrees F.

Step 2: Stir 2 tablespoons oil, 1 tablespoon oregano, half the garlic, 1/4 teaspoon pepper and 1/8 teaspoon salt together in a large bowl. Add Brussels sprouts, gnocchi and onion; toss to coat. Spread on a large rimmed baking sheet.

Step 3: Stir 1 tablespoon oil, the remaining 1 tablespoon oregano, the remaining garlic and the remaining 1/4 teaspoon pepper and 1/8 teaspoon salt in the large bowl. Add chicken and toss to coat. Nestle the chicken into the vegetable mixture. Roast for 10 minutes.

Step 4: Remove from the oven and add the tomatoes; stir to combine. Continue roasting until the Brussels sprouts are tender and the chicken is just cooked through, about 10 minutes more. Stir vinegar and the remaining 1 tablespoon oil into the vegetable mixture.

Nutrition Facts

Serving Size: 1 chicken thigh & 1 1/2 cups vegetables each

Per Serving: 604 calories; protein 39.1g; carbohydrates 60.6g; dietary fiber 6.8g; sugars 4.8g; fat 23.9g; saturated fat 4.7g; cholesterol 154.3mg; vitamin a iu 1224.4IU; vitamin c 104.1mg; folate 89.7mcg; calcium 96.8mg; iron 3.8mg; magnesium 66mg; potassium 913.8mg; sodium 657.3mg; thiamin 0.3mg.

Chickpea & Quinoa Bowl with Roasted Red Pepper Sauce

Prep Time:	20 minutes
Cook Time:	20 minutes
Servings	4

Ingredients

- 1 (7 ounce) jar roasted red peppers, rinsed
- ¼ cup slivered almonds
- 4 tablespoons extra-virgin olive oil, divided
- 1 small clove garlic, minced
- 1 teaspoon paprika
- ½ teaspoon ground cumin
- ¼ teaspoon crushed red pepper (optional)
- 2 cups cooked quinoa
- ¼ cup Kalamata olives, chopped
- ¼ cup finely chopped red onion
- 1 (15 ounce) can chickpeas, rinsed
- 1 cup diced cucumber
- ¼ cup crumbled feta cheese
- 2 tablespoons finely chopped fresh parsley

Preparation

Step 1: Place peppers, almonds, 2 tablespoons oil, garlic, paprika, cumin and crushed red pepper (if using) in a mini food processor. Puree until fairly smooth.

Step 2: Combine quinoa, olives, red onion and the remaining 2 tablespoons oil in a medium bowl.

Step 3: To serve, divide the quinoa mixture among 4 bowls and top with equal amounts of the chickpeas, cucumber and the red pepper sauce. Sprinkle with feta and parsley.

Nutrition Facts

Serving Size: 1 1/2 cups

Per Serving: 479 calories; protein 12.7g; carbohydrates 49.5g; dietary fiber 7.7g; sugars 2.5g; fat 24.8g; saturated fat 4.3g; cholesterol 8.3mg; vitamin a iu 1145.8IU; vitamin c 9.6mg; folate 105.8mcg; calcium 135.8mg; iron 3.5mg; magnesium 109.9mg; potassium 442.6mg; sodium 646mg; thiamin 0.2mg.

Garlic Roasted Salmon & Brussels Sprouts

Prep Time: 45 minutes
Servings 6

Ingredients

- 14 large cloves garlic, divided
- ¼ cup extra-virgin olive oil
- 2 tablespoons finely chopped fresh oregano, divided
- 1 teaspoon salt, divided
- ¾ teaspoon freshly ground pepper, divided
- 6 cups Brussels sprouts, trimmed and sliced
- ¾ cup white wine, preferably Chardonnay
- 2 pounds wild-caught salmon fillet, skinned, cut into 6 portions
- Lemon wedges

Preparation

Step 1: Preheat oven to 450 degrees F.

Step 2: Mince 2 garlic cloves and combine in a small bowl with oil, 1 tablespoon oregano, 1/2 teaspoon salt and 1/4 teaspoon pepper. Halve the remaining garlic and toss with Brussels sprouts and 3 tablespoons of the seasoned oil in a large roasting pan. Roast, stirring once, for 15 minutes.

Step 3: Add wine to the remaining oil mixture. Remove the pan from oven, stir the vegetables and place salmon on top. Drizzle with the wine mixture. Sprinkle with the remaining 1 tablespoon oregano and 1/2 teaspoon each salt and pepper. Bake until the salmon is just cooked through, 5 to 10 minutes more. Serve with lemon wedges.

Nutrition Facts

Per Serving: 334 calories; protein 33.1g; carbohydrates 10.3g; dietary fiber 2.7g; sugars 2g; fat 15.4g; saturated fat 2.8g; cholesterol 70.7mg; vitamin a iu 989.8IU; vitamin c 64.3mg; folate 74.8mcg; calcium 115.4mg; iron 2.2mg; magnesium 67.8mg; potassium 921.3mg; sodium 485mg; thiamin 0.2mg.

Salmon Pita Sandwich

Prep Time: 10 minutes
Servings 1

Ingredients

- 2 tablespoons plain nonfat yogurt
- 2 teaspoons chopped fresh dill
- 2 teaspoons lemon juice
- ½ teaspoon prepared horseradish
- 3 ounces flaked drained canned sockeye salmon
- ½ 6-inch whole-wheat pita bread
- ½ cup watercress

Preparation

Step 1: Combine yogurt, dill, lemon juice and horseradish in a small bowl; stir in salmon. Stuff the pita half with the salmon salad and watercress.

Nutrition Facts

Serving Size: 1 sandwich

Per Serving: 239 calories; protein 24.8g; carbohydrates 19g; dietary fiber 2.3g; sugars 3g; fat 7.1g; saturated fat 1.4g; cholesterol 67.8mg; vitamin a iu 414.1IU; vitamin c 8.2mg; folate 21.6mcg; calcium 273.8mg; iron 1.5mg; magnesium 54.7mg; potassium 436.1mg; sodium 510.2mg; thiamin 0.2mg.

Quinoa & Chia Oatmeal Mix

Prep Time: 10 minutes
Servings 12

Ingredients

- 2 cups old-fashioned rolled oats
- 1 cup rolled wheat and/or barley flakes (see Tip)
- 1 cup quinoa
- 1 cup dried fruit, such as raisins, cranberries and/or chopped apricots
- ½ cup chia and/or hemp seeds
- 1 teaspoon ground cinnamon
- ¾ teaspoon salt

Preparation

Step 1: To make the hot cereal dry mix: Combine oats, wheat and/or barley flakes, quinoa, dried fruit, seeds, cinnamon and salt in an airtight container.

Step 2: To make 1 serving of hot cereal: Combine 1/3 cup Quinoa & Chia Oatmeal Mix with 1 1/4 cups water (or milk) in a small saucepan. Bring to a boil. Reduce heat, partially cover and simmer, stirring occasionally, until thickened, 12 to 15 minutes. Let stand, covered, for 5 minutes. Stir in a sweetener of your choice and top with nuts and/or more dried fruit, if desired. Makes 1 cup.

Nutrition Facts

Serving Size: 1/3 cup dry mix

Per Serving: 196 calories; protein 6.2g; carbohydrates 35.5g; dietary fiber 6.1g; sugars 8.2g; fat 4.2g; saturated fat 0.5g; vitamin a iu 6.4IU; vitamin c 0.4mg; folate 36.6mcg; calcium 59.1mg; iron 2.3mg; magnesium 91.3mg; potassium 247.4mg; sodium 148.5mg; thiamin 0.2mg.

Skillet Lemon Chicken & Potatoes with Kale

Prep Time: 50 minutes
Servings: 4

Ingredients

- 3 tablespoons extra-virgin olive oil, divided
- 1 pound boneless, skinless chicken thighs, trimmed
- ½ teaspoon salt, divided
- **½ teaspoon ground pepper, divided**
- 1 pound baby Yukon Gold potatoes, halved lengthwise
- ½ cup low-sodium chicken broth
- 1 large lemon, sliced and seeds removed
- 4 cloves garlic, minced
- 1 tablespoon chopped fresh tarragon
- 6 cups baby kale

Preparation

Step 1: Preheat oven to 400°F.

Step 2: Heat 1 tablespoon oil in a large cast-iron skillet over medium-high heat. Sprinkle chicken with 1/4 teaspoon each salt and pepper. Cook, turning once, until browned on both sides, about 5 minutes total. Transfer to a plate.

Step 3: Add the remaining 2 tablespoons oil, potatoes and the remaining 1/4 teaspoon each salt and pepper to the pan. Cook the potatoes, cut-side down, until browned, about 3 minutes. Stir in broth, lemon, garlic and tarragon. Return the chicken to the pan.

Step 4: Transfer the pan to the oven. Roast until the chicken is cooked through and the potatoes are tender, about 15 minutes. Stir kale into the mixture and roast until it has wilted, 3 to 4 minutes.

Equipment

Large cast-iron skillet

Nutrition Facts

Serving Size: 1 chicken thigh & 1 cup vegetables

Per Serving: 374 calories; protein 24.7g; carbohydrates 25.6g; dietary fiber 2.9g; sugars 1.8g; fat 19.3g; saturated fat 3.9g; cholesterol 75.5mg; vitamin a iu 2463.4IU; vitamin c 40.6mg; folate 51mcg; calcium 64.8mg; iron 2mg; magnesium 53mg; potassium 677.3mg; sodium 377.9mg; thiamin 0.2mg.

Fattoush Salad

Prep Time: 20 minutes
Servings 6

Ingredients

- 2 loaves pita bread
- Extra virgin olive oil
- Kosher salt
- 2 tsp sumac, divided, more as needed
- 1 heart of Romaine lettuce, chopped
- 1 English cucumber, cut in half, seeds scraped, then chopped or sliced into half moons
- 5 Roma tomatoes, chopped
- 5 green onions (both white and green parts), chopped
- 5 radishes, stems removed, thinly sliced
- 2 cups chopped fresh parsley leaves, stems removed
- 1 cup chopped fresh mint leaves (optional)

Vinaigrette/Dressing

- Juice of 1 lemon or 1 ½ limes
- ⅓ cup extra virgin olive oil
- 1 to 2 tablespoons pomegranate molasses, optional
- Salt and pepper
- 1 tsp sumac
- ¼ tsp ground cinnamon
- Scant ¼ tsp ground allspice

Preparation

1. Break the pita bread into small bite-size pieces. Heat 3 tablespoon of olive oil in a large pan until shimmering, and add the pita bread. Fry briefly until browned, tossing frequently. Using a pair of tongs, transfer the fried pita chips to a plate lined with paper towel to drain. Season with salt, pepper and sumac.
2. In a large mixing bowl, combine the chopped lettuce, cucumber, tomatoes, green onions with the sliced radish and parsley.
3. To make the dressing, in a small bowl, whisk together the lemon or lime juice, olive oil, pomegranate molasses (if using), salt, pepper and spices.
4. Pour toss lightly. Finally, add the pita chips, and more sumac if you like, and toss one more time. Transfer to small serving bowls or plates. Enjoy!

Nutrition fact

Total Fat 20.4g 26% Saturated Fat 3g Trans Fat 0g Sodium 177.6mg 8% Total Carbohydrate 39.8g 14% Sugars 11.4g Protein 9.1g 18% Vitamin A63%Vitamin C61%Calcium17%Iron37%Magnesium26%Potassium26%Zinc16%Phosphorus16%Thiamin (B1)25%Riboflavin (B2)30%Niacin (B3)19%Vitamin B630%Folic Acid (B9)58%Vitamin E12%Vitamin K296%

Bourtheto Fish Stew Greek

Fish Stew With Cod

Prep Time: 5 minutes
Cook time 30 minutes
Servings 2-4

Ingredients

- 4 cod fillets
- 1 1/4 cups onion, sliced (or diced if you like)
- 1 cup water
- 1/4 cup olive oil
- 1/2 teaspoon paprika
- 1/8 teaspoon cayenne
- 1 teaspoon salt
- 1 teaspoon pepper

Preparation

1. In pan add: water, olive oil, onions, paprika, cayenne, salt and pepper.
2. Bring to boil, reduce heat and simmer for 10-15min, until onions soften.
3. Add cod and continue simmering for another 10-15min or until fish is done.
4. Place desired number of fish in each dish, top with onion mixture.
5. Serve!

Lemon Garlic Shrimp Pasta

Prep Time: 10 minutes
Cook time 10 minutes
Servings 4

Ingredients

- 12 ounces dried spaghetti or other long, thin pasta
- 3 tablespoons olive oil
- 2 tablespoons butter
- 5 large garlic cloves minced
- ¼ teaspoon crushed red pepper flakes or more
- 1 pound medium shrimp peeled and deveined
- 1 large lemon juice and zest
- ⅓ cup chopped fresh parsley
- Kosher salt and freshly ground black pepper to taste
- 2 ounces parmesan cheese freshly grated, optional

Preparation

1. Bring a large pot of salted water to boil. Cook pasta in boiling water until firm to the bite (al dente), about 8 minutes. Drain, reserving 1 cup of pasta water.
2. Meanwhile, heat olive oil and butter in a large skillet over medium-high heat until sizzling. Add minced garlic and red pepper flakes; cook and stir until fragrant, about 30 seconds. Add shrimp; cook and stir until shrimp is just cooked through, 3 to 4 minutes. Remove from heat.
3. Once you've drained the pasta, set skillet with the shrimp mixture over medium heat. Add drained, cooked pasta and ¼ cup of reserved pasta water; toss to coat. Cook and stir until heated through, adding more pasta water if pasta seems too dry.
4. Remove pasta from heat and stir in fresh lemon juice and zest, and parsley. Season to taste with salt and pepper. Transfer to serving bowl or platter; top with grated parmesan cheese if using and serve.

Nutrition fact

Calories: 643kcal Carbohydrates: 68g Protein: 40g Fat: 23g Saturated Fat: 8g Cholesterol: 310mg Sodium: 1170mg Potassium: 373mg Fiber: 4g Sugar: 3g Vitamin A: 744IU Vitamin C: 27mg Calcium: 371mg Iron: 4mg

Mushroom Chorizo and Halloumi Tacos

Prep Time: 20 minutes
Cook time 40 minutes
Servings 8

Ingredients

- 500 g button mushrooms, wiped clean, cut into quarters
- 3 tablespoon olive oil
- 1 teaspoon salt
- 1 teaspoon black pepper
- 1 pinch oregano, dried and Greek preferably
- 125 g chorizo sausage, (cooked chorizo not fresh)
- 200 g haloumi cheese, sliced in half
- 8 tortillas, medium-sized and warmed in a pan
- 1 tablespoon chilies, finely chopped
- 1 tablespoon coriander, finely chopped

Preparation

1. Combine the mushrooms, olive oil, salt, pepper and oregano in a bowl. Place on baking tray and cook in a 200 deg C oven for 30-35 mins. Remove and set aside and allow to cool slightly.
2. Preheat a little oil in a pan cook the chorizo on a medium high heat for a few mins until crispy. Remove and set aside.
3. In the same pan pan fry the halloumi for 2 mins each side until, browned and soft. Once cooked cut the haloumi into small even slices.
4. Combine the mushrooms, chorizo and haloumi in a separate bowl.
5. To make a taco place a 2-3 tbsps of the mushroom mixture into a warmed tortilla. Garnish with fresh chilies and coriander and serve immediately.\

Nutrition fact

Calories: 302 kcal | Carbohydrates: 18 g | Protein: 14 g | Fat: 20 g | Saturated Fat: 8 g

Falafel Pita Sandwich

Prep Time: 40 minutes
Cook time   10 minutes
Servings   20

Ingredients

Ingredients for the Falafels

- 2 cups dried chickpeas
- 4 garlic cloves finely chopped
- 1 small onion finely chopped
- 1 cup broccoli florets
- ¾ cups fresh coriander chopped
- ½ cup parsley chopped
- 1 teaspoon coriander powder
- 1 teaspoon cumin powder
- 1 teaspoon black pepper
- 1 teaspoon salt add more to taste

Ingredients for the Falafel Sandwich

- Pita bread
- Hummus
- 1 large tomato
- ½ cucumber
- Green or black olives
- Sambal or hot sauce optional

Preparation

1. Leave the chickpeas soaking overnight, at least 12 hours before preparing your falafels.
2. Once your chickpeas have been soaking for at least 12 hours, rinse them and remove the excess of water. Add them in a food processor and blend for a couple of seconds.
3. Add to the food processor the onion, broccoli, fresh coriander, fresh parsley, coriander powder, cumin powder, black pepper and salt.
4. Blend all the Ingredients until you have a well-combined mixture. It shouldn't be mushy as the balls will be too dense, but it needs to be blended enough for the dough to not fall apart when frying them.
5. Using your hands or using a falafel press, form the dough into round shapes. Make sure the size is not too small or too big. It should be around the size of your palm.
6. Heat up some neutral oil in a small frying pan so you don't have to use that much oil. Fry the falafels until they are brown and crispy on the outside. If the falafels are shaped correctly, not much oil will go inside. The inside part will still be really fresh and light.
7. Cut the Pita Bread in half, spread some hummus and spicy sauce (optional) on the bread, add some fresh chopped tomatoes and cucumber drizzled with some olive oil, add lettuce and finally the homemade falafels. Top the sandwich with green or black olives. Optionally, can add some yoghurt sauce as well.

Nutrition

Calories: 82kcal | Carbohydrates: 14g | Protein: 4g | Fat: 1g | Saturated Fat: 1g | Sodium: 125mg | Potassium: 243mg | Fiber: 4g | Sugar: 3g | Vitamin A: 269IU | Vitamin C: 9mg | Calcium: 33mg | Iron: 2mg

Zucchini blossoms stuffed with bulgur

Prep Time: 90 minutes
Servings 8-10

Ingredients:
- 20-25 zucchini blossoms
- 1 cup olive oil
- 1 onion
- 3 scallions
- 3 cloves garlic, minced
- 1 cup grated zucchini (1-2 zucchini)
- 1 cup bulgur (cracked wheat)
- 1/2-1 tsp fresh chili pepper, or 1/3-1/2 tsp dried red pepper flakes
- 1 1/2 cups water
- 3 sprigs chopped fresh mint
- 1 bunch chopped fresh dill
- Sea salt and freshly ground pepper
- 1/2 cup pine nuts (optional)
- 2/3 cup raisins (optional)
- 3 cups strained plain yogurt

Preparation:
1. Finely chop the fresh dill and mint.
2. Chop the onion and scallions in brunoise.
3. Grate the zucchini.
4. Preheat the oven to 375° F.
5. In a deep skillet, heat half the oil over medium heat and sauté the onion, scallions, and garlic until soft (about 5 minutes).
6. Add the zucchini, bulgur, raisins, chili pepper, and 1 cup water. Reduce the heat and simmer for 10 minutes
7. Add a little more water if all is absorbed. Turn off the heat and add the pine nuts, mint, and dill to the stuffing.
8. Season with salt, stir, and taste. Add more salt and pepper if needed.
9. Using a spoon, carefully stuff each blossom. Fold the top over and place on their sides, very closely together, in an earthenware casserole.
10. Pour in the remaining olive oil and 1/2 cup water. Cover the dish and place in the oven. Bake for about 1 hour, checking periodically to see if a little more water is needed, until most of the liquid has been absorbed.
11. Serve hot or cold, accompanied by yogurt

Warm spiced eggplant and chickpea salad

Prep Time: 10 minutes
Cook time 20 minutes
Servings 4

Ingredients

- 2 tablespoon olive oil

1 eggplant, cut in 2cm cubes

- 150-gram button mushrooms, quartered
- 2 tablespoon harissa or mild chilli paste
- 2 clove garlic, crushed
- 400 gram can diced tomatoes
- 400 gram can chickpeas, drained, rinsed
- 50-gram baby spinach leaves
- 1/4 cup roughly chopped parsley leaves
- 2 crusty bread rolls, torn

Preparation

1. Heat oil in a large frying pan on medium. Fry eggplant 4-5 minutes, shaking pan occasionally, until golden all over. Add mushroom and sauté for 3-4 minutes. Stir in harissa and garlic and cook for 1 minute.
2. Add tomatoes and chickpeas. Bring to boil. Reduce heat to low. Simmer, covered, 8-10 minutes.
3. When ready to serve, toss spinach leaves and parsley through. Season to taste. Serve with torn crusty bread rolls.

Tabbouleh

Prep Time: 30 minutes
Servings 8

Ingredients

- 1 cup bulghur wheat
- 1 1/2 cups boiling water
- 1/4 cup freshly squeezed lemon juice (2 lemons)
- 1/4 cup good olive oil
- 3 1/2 teaspoons kosher salt
- 1 cup minced scallions, white and green parts (1 bunch)
- 1 cup chopped fresh mint leaves (1 bunch)
- 1 cup chopped flat-leaf parsley (1 bunch)
- 1 hothouse cucumber, unpeeled, seeded, and medium-diced
- 2 cups cherry tomatoes, cut in half
- 1 teaspoon freshly ground black pepper

Preparation

1. Place the bulghur in a large bowl, pour in the boiling water, and add the lemon juice, olive oil, and 1 1/2 teaspoons salt. Stir, then allow to stand at room temperature for about 1 hour.
2. Add the scallions, mint, parsley, cucumber, tomatoes, 2 teaspoons salt, and the pepper; mix well. Season, to taste, and serve or cover and refrigerate. The flavor will improve if the tabbouleh sits for a few hours.

Louvi – Black eyed Peas

Prep Time: 15 minutes
Cook time 60 minutes
Servings 5

Ingredients

- 250 grams black eyed beans
- 1 bunch of silver beet orchard (about 3 cups)
- 1 medium onion, finely chopped
- 1 spring onion, finely chopped
- 1 clove garlic, finely chopped
- 1/4 cup olive oil
- 2 – 3 tablespoons parsley, finely chopped
- 1 tablespoon, dill or fennel fronds
- Salt (with moderation)
- Freshly ground black pepper
- 4 cups water
- 1/3 cup lemon juice
- 1 tsp flour
- 2 - 3 tbsp parsley, finely chopped
- 1 tbsp dill, finely chopped

Preparation

1. Put blackeyed beans in a pot with water and boil for 15 minutes and drain.
2. Meantime, wash and cut silver beet in smaller pieces.
3. Sauté the onion and garlic with olive oil and then add silver beet and stir.
4. Add the black-eyed peas and season with salt and pepper. Add water to cover all Ingredients.
5. Bring to boil, reduce the heat and simmer until the beans are soft.
6. Toward the end add the parsley and dill and mix.
7. Dissolve the flour in the lemon juice and add it to the mixture. Cook for a few more minutes.

Nutrition fact

Calories 132.72 Total Fat 11.07g Saturated Fat 1.56g Sodium 739.05mg Carbohydrates 8.7g Fiber 2.55g sugar 3.35g Protein 1.86g

Greek Okra Stew Recipe with Tomatoes (Bamies Laderes)

Prep Time: 30 minutes
Cook time: 40 minutes
Servings: 4

Ingredients

For the Greek Okra stew (Bamies)

- 450g okra (frozen)
- 2 medium potatoes
- 2 spring onions
- 1/2 red onion
- 1 clove of garlic
- 1 carrot
- 50ml olive oil
- 1 teaspoon tomato paste
- 40g white wine
- 400g canned tomatoes
- 100g vegetable stock
- 300ml water
- 2 tablespoons parsley, chopped
- 2 teaspoons sugar
- Salt and pepper

To serve

- Oregano
- 150 g feta cheese

Preparation

1. To prepare this traditional Greek okra stew recipe, start by preparing the vegetables. First cut the potatoes into cubes. Slice the carrot and spring onions and chop the red onion and garlic.
2. Heat a pot over high heat and add in the olive oil and the all of the vegetables and the potatoes. Sauté over high heat until they caramelise and become tender, for about 3-4 minutes. Then add the tomato paste and sauté for 1-2 more minutes.
3. Pour in the white wine and deglaze. Wait for the wine to evaporate and then add the tomatoes, the okra, stock, water, sugar, parsley and season. Stir with a wooden spoon and put the lid on. Simmer the okra stew for about 30 minutes at low heat, until tender.
4. Serve this Greek okra stew with crumbled feta cheese and a pinch of dried oregano. Enjoy!

Nutrition

Serving Size: 1 plate Calories: 341kcalsugar: 10.6gsodium: 1133mgfat: 20.5gsaturated Fat: 7.4gunsaturated Fat: 12gtrans Fat: 0gcarbohydrates: 31.9gfiber: 8.4gprotein: 10.2gcholesterol: 33.4mg

Hummus

Prep Time: 20 minutes
Cook time: 20 minutes
Servings: 8

Ingredients

- 1 can (15 ounces) chickpeas, rinsed and drained, or 1 ½ cups cooked chickpeas
- ½ teaspoon baking soda (if you're using canned chickpeas)
- ¼ cup lemon juice (from 1 ½ to 2 lemons), more to taste
- 1 medium-to-large clove garlic, roughly chopped
- ½ teaspoon fine sea salt, to taste
- ½ cup tahini
- 2 to 4 tablespoons ice water, more as needed
- ½ teaspoon ground cumin
- 1 tablespoon extra-virgin olive oil
- Any of the following garnishes: drizzle of olive oil or zhoug sauce, sprinkle of ground sumac or paprika, chopped fresh parsley

Preparation

1. Place the chickpeas in a medium saucepan and add the baking soda. Cover the chickpeas by several inches of water, then bring the mixture to a boil over high heat. Continue boiling, reducing heat if necessary, to prevent overflow, for about 20 minutes, or until the chickpeas look bloated, their skins are falling off, and they're quite soft. In a fine-mesh strainer, drain the chickpeas and run cool water over them for about 30 seconds. Set aside (no need to peel the chickpeas for this recipe!).
2. Meanwhile, in a food processor or high-powered blender, combine the lemon juice, garlic and salt. Process until the garlic is very finely chopped, then let the mixture rest so the garlic flavor can mellow, ideally 10 minutes or longer.
3. Add the tahini to the food processor and blend until the mixture is thick and creamy, stopping to scrape down any tahini stuck to the sides and bottom of the processor as necessary.
4. While running the food processor, drizzle in 2 tablespoons ice water. Scrape down the food processor, and blend until the mixture is ultra-smooth, pale and creamy. (If your tahini was extra-thick to begin with, you might need to add 1 to 2 tablespoons more ice water.)
5. Add the cumin and the drained, over-cooked chickpeas to the food processor. While blending, drizzle in the olive oil. Blend until the mixture is super smooth, scraping down the sides of the processor as necessary, about 2 minutes. Add more ice water by the tablespoon if necessary, to achieve a super creamy texture.
6. Taste, and adjust as necessary—I almost always add another ¼ teaspoon salt for more overall flavor and another tablespoon of lemon juice for extra zing.
7. Scrape the hummus into a serving bowl or platter, and use a spoon to create nice swooshes on top. Top with garnishes of your choice, and serve. Leftover hummus keeps well in the refrigerator, covered, for up to 1 week.

Grilled Swordfish with Lemon and Caper Sauce

Prep Time: 20 minutes
Cook time 12 minutes
Servings 6

Ingredients

- 4 tablespoons unsalted butter
- 1 large lemon, peeled, cut crosswise into 8 1/4" slices, seeded, with all the juice
- 2 tablespoons drained nonpareil capers
- Sea salt and freshly ground white pepper to taste
- 3 swordfish steaks cut 1 1/4-inch thick (about 1 pound each)
- 3 tablespoons (very green) extra-virgin olive oil
- 2 teaspoons finely chopped parsley for garnish

Preparation

1. Melt 4 tablespoons butter in a small saucepan over medium low heat. Stir constantly until the butter is light brown, about 3 minutes.
2. Cut the lemon slices into quarters. Add them (with their juice), and the capers, to the saucepan. Reduce the heat and cook, shaking the pan several times, until the lemon and capers are heated through, about 1 minute. Taste for and correct seasoning.
3. Light a grill or preheat the broiler. Brush the swordfish with olive oil on both sides. Sprinkle with salt and freshly ground white pepper to taste.
4. Grill or broil the swordfish about 4 inches from the heat, turning once, until charred outside and still slightly pink in the center (3 to 4 minutes per side).
5. Transfer the swordfish to a large platter and cut into thick strips. Pour the lemon and caper sauce over the fish and serve immediately, garnished with the chopped parsley.
6. Wine Tip: Juicy whites are most refreshing in summer. There are a whole host of tasty and affordable bottles in that category. We drank Albariño from Martin Codax (and also toasted Spain's win in the World Cup!)

Chicken Tagine with Apricots and Almonds

Prep Time:	30 minutes
Cook time	45-50 minutes
Servings	4

Ingredients

- 1.5kg free-range chicken, cut into 8 pieces, or 8 thighs
- 1-2 tbsp olive oil
- 2 onions, finely sliced
- 2 garlic cloves, crushed
- Pinch of saffron threads
- 1 tsp each turmeric, ground cumin and ground cinnamon
- 1½ tsp ground ginger
- 1½ tsp hot paprika
- 500ml apple juice
- 500ml chicken stock, hot
- 250g ready-to-eat dried apricots
- 100g whole peeled almonds
- Large bunch of fresh mint, chopped
- Large bunch of fresh coriander or parsley, chopped

Preparation

1. In a heavy-based flameproof casserole, lightly brown the chicken in the olive oil over a medium heat. Reduce the heat, add the onion and garlic and sauté for 3-4 minutes.
2. Add the spices, cook for 2 minutes, then pour in the apple juice and stock to cover the meat. Bring to
3. The boil and simmer for 15 minutes, stirring occasionally.
4. Add the apricots and almonds and cook for a further 15 minutes until the chicken is tender and the liquid has reduced and thickened.
5. Before serving, stir in most of the herbs, keeping some as a garnish.

Nutrition fact

CALORIES 462KCALS FAT 19.3G (2.7G SATURATED) PROTEIN 56G CARBOHYDRATES 19.8G (16.3G SUGARS) SALT 0.8G

Lentil Kale Soup

Prep Time: 10 minutes
Cook time: 45 minutes
Servings: 4

Ingredients

- 1 tablespoon olive oil
- 1 large onion chopped
- 2 garlic cloves minced
- 2 large carrots chopped
- 2 celery ribs chopped
- 1 ½ cup dried green lentils
- 1 teaspoon cumin
- ½ teaspoon coriander
- 1 teaspoon Kosher salt
- ½ teaspoon black pepper
- 6 cups vegetable broth
- 2-3 cups kale destemmed, roughly chopped

Preparation

1. In a large pot, heat olive over medium high heat. Add onions and cook until translucent, about 3-5 minutes. Add the garlic, carrots and celery and cook for an additional 2-3 minutes.
2. Add the green lentils, cumin, coriander, salt and pepper and cook with the vegetables to lightly toast the lentils, about 5 minutes. Add vegetable broth and bring to a boil; reduce heat and then simmer on low for 30 minutes until the lentils are cooked and the broth thickens.
3. Stir in the kale and continue to simmer until the kale wilts, about 2 more minutes.
4. Remove from heat and serve immediately.

Nutrition

Calories: 221kcal, Carbohydrates: 36g, Protein: 13g, Fat: 3g, Saturated Fat: 1g, Sodium: 1355mg, Potassium: 637mg, Fiber: 15g, Sugar: 5g, Vitamin A: 6146IU, Vitamin C: 32mg, Calcium: 75mg, Iron: 4mg

Saffron Fish Sauce

Prep Time: 5 minutes
Cook time 10 minutes
Servings 2

Ingredients

- 2000ml Fish Stock
- 500ml Cream
- 200ml White Wine
- 20g Fresh Parsley
- 70g Shallot
- 30ml Rapeseed Oil
- 2g Thyme
- 3 Garlic Cloves
- Pinch of Saffron

Allergens

- Fish Milk Sulphites

Preparation

1. Boil the stock on a high heat until it has reduced to a 1/4 of it's original.
2. Reduce the heat, add the cream and then bring back to the boil.
3. In a separate pan, sweat shallots, garlic and thyme in oil, add white wine and saffron and reduce by at least half.
4. Add fish cream sauce and boil together for a few minutes until taste and consistency is achieved.
5. A small reduction may occur with the cream sauce.

Nutrition fact

Per 100g 371cal / 1533kj Fat 34g Saturates 19g Carbs 8.2g Sugars 2.5g Protein 5.1g Salt 0.47

Bar bunya Pinaki (Turkish Baked Beans)

Prep Time: 30 minutes
Cook time 40 minutes
Servings 8

Ingredients

- 1 c dried borlotti or pinto beans, soaked overnight
- 1 Tbsp olive oil
- 1 onion, diced
- 2 garlic cloves, minced
- 2 carrots, diced
- 2 large tomatoes, diced, or 1 (14oz can) diced tomatoes, with juices
- 1 Tbsp tomato paste
- 1 tsp sugar
- ½ tsp salt
- ¼ tsp ground black pepper
- 1 – 1 ½ c water
- Fresh parsley and lemon wedges (for serving)

Preparation

1. Add soaked and drained beans to a large saucepan and cover with one inch of water. Bring the beans to a boil and reduce the heat to medium low. Simmer the beans until just tender, 20-30 minutes.
2. In a large skillet, heat olive oil. Add the onion and garlic. Sauté for 2-3 minutes over medium heat, until soft. Add the carrots and sauté 5 min. Add the tomatoes, tomato paste, sugar, salt, and pepper. Mix well.
3. Add the cooked, drained beans and fresh water (use 1 ½ c of water if using fresh tomatoes or 1 c of water if using canned tomatoes with juices). Mix well and simmer, uncovered over medium-low heat, until most of the liquid has evaporated, 30 minutes, stirring occasionally.
4. The dish can be served immediately or refrigerated and served cold. (The flavors of this dish do improve over time, so don't be afraid to prepare it up to 24 hours ahead of time.)
5. To serve, garnish beans with chopped fresh parsley and lemon slice.

Nutrition

Serving: 1g | Calories: 124kcal | Carbohydrates: 20.8g | Fat: 2.2g | Sodium: 166mg | Fiber: 5.1g | Sugar: 3.8g

Zesty Eggplant Frittata

Prep Time: 20 minutes
Cook time 35 minutes
Servings 6

Ingredients

- 1 medium eggplant, cubed
- 2 cups (500 ml) cherry or grape tomatoes (1 pint), halved
- ½ cup (125 ml) pitted olives, halved
- 1 small onion, coarsely chopped
- 2 cloves garlic, sliced
- 3 tbsp (45 ml) olive oil
- 2 tsp (10 ml) red wine vinegar
- ½ tsp (2.5 ml) dried oregano
- ½ tsp (2.5 ml) hot pepper flakes
- 1/8 tsp (0.5 ml) pepper
- 8 eggs
- ⅓ cup (75 ml) chopped fresh parsley
- ¼ cup (60 ml) water

Preparation

1. Combine eggplant, cherry tomatoes, olives, onion, garlic, oil, vinegar, oregano, hot pepper flakes and pepper in large bowl; toss gently to combine. Spoon mixture onto large baking sheet; spread evenly.
2. Roast in preheated 425°F (220°C) oven, stirring halfway through cooking time, until vegetables are tender and lightly browned, 25 to 30 minutes. Remove from oven. Leave oven on.
3. Whisk eggs, parsley and water. Lightly spray 10 or 12-inch (25 or 30 cm) non-stick ovenproof skillet with cooking spray. Heat skillet over medium heat. Pour egg mixture into skillet. As eggs set around edge of skillet, with spatula, gently lift cooked portions to allow uncooked egg to flow underneath. Cook until bottom is set and surface is still somewhat liquid, 6 or 7 minutes.
4. Remove skillet from heat; spoon eggplant and tomato mixture over top of frittata. Return to oven and bake until egg mixture is set, about 10 minutes.

Italian Calamari Salad

Prep Time: 28 minutes
Cook time 2 minutes
Servings 4

Ingredients

Mix together in bowl

- 1-pound calamari cleaned, tubes cut into ½" circles and tentacles left whole
- 1 teaspoon baking soda
- 1 teaspoon kosher salt
- Water enough to cover calamari in bowl

For the salad

- 1 cup celery or roughly 2 ribs - thinly sliced on a bias
- ½ cup red roasted peppers chopped
- ½ cup Sicilian green olives pitted and sliced
- ¼ cup red onion diced
- 1 clove garlic grated
- ¼ cup parsley minced
- 4 tablespoons lemon juice plus more to taste
- ½ cup extra virgin olive oil plus more to taste
- Salt to taste
- ¼ teaspoon crushed red pepper flakes

Preparation

1. Rinse and clean calamari then cut into rings and cut any large tentacles in half. Mix calamari with salt, baking soda, and enough water to cover and set aside for 15 minutes.
2. Place celery, red roasted peppers, olives, onion, garlic, parsley, crushed red pepper, lemon juice, and olive oil into a large bowl and mix together.
3. Set up a bowl of ice water and bring a large pot of water to boil.
4. Drain calamari well then boil in water for two minutes or until cooked through. Using a slotted spoon, place cooked calamari in the ice water bath immediately.
5. Once calamari is cold, drain and then add to the bowl of veggies and mix together. Taste test and season with salt to taste.
6. Chill the calamari salad in the fridge for at least a couple of hours. Before serving, taste test and add more olive oil, lemon juice, or salt and pepper if required. Enjoy!

Greek Spinach and Rice Recipe (Spanakorizo)

Prep Time:	10 minutes
Cook time	20 minutes
Servings	8

Ingredients

- 1kg fresh or frozen spinach, rinsed and stemmed (35 oz.)
- 200g rice white rice (7 oz.)
- 1/2 cup olive oil
- 4 spring onions, chopped
- 1 red onion, finely chopped
- 1 leek, sliced
- 1/2 bunch dill, finely chopped
- 150g tinned chopped tomatoes (5.5 oz.) Or 200g of fresh tomatoes, if in season.
- 1 tbsp tomato paste
- 1 cube vegetable stock
- Salt and freshly ground pepper

Preparation

1. To prepare this spanakorizo recipe (Greek spinach and rice), heat the olive oil in a large skillet over medium high heat. Add the onions, spring onions and leek and sauté for 3-4 minutes, until translucent.
2. Add the spinach and cook stirring for a few minutes, until wilted. Stir in the tomatoes, the tomato paste, two cups of hot water, the vegetable stock, the rice and season. Reduce heat to low and simmer, covered, for about 20-25 minutes, until the rice is tender.
3. While the Spanakorizo is simmering away, stir it every so often and check if the pan appears to be getting dry. If it is, add some more hot water and stir.
4. To know when it's ready, take a grain of rice out of the skillet and pinch it with your fingernails. If its white on the inside it needs a little bit longer. When it's close to ready, season with salt and pepper to taste. Finally, finish the spanakorizo with fresh chopped dill and cook for a a couple more minutes.
5. Serve this traditional Greek spinach and rice (spanakorizo) with a squeeze of a lemon and top with crumbled feta. Enjoy!

Nutrition

Serving Size: 1 plate Calories: 199kcalsugar: 2.2gsodium: 416mgfat: 14.7gsaturated Fat: 2.1gunsaturated Fat: 11.8gtrans Fat: 0gcarbohydrates: 15.7gfiber: 3.7gprotein: 4.8gcholesterol: 0mg

Foraged Greens with Garlic And Paprika (Tsigarelli)

Prep Time: 20 minutes
Cook time 15 minutes

Ingredients

- 16 oz mixed wild greens especially purslane, dandelions, and nettles, if available
- 2 large cloves garlic finely chopped or grated
- 1 small 4 oz white onion, diced
- 2 oz spring onions sliced ¼ inch
- 4 oz wild fennel greens stems removed
- Small handful fresh chopped mint or dill optional but recommended
- 5 Tablespoons extra virgin olive oil
- 4 teaspoons mild paprika
- Pinch of cayenne pepper or crushed red pepper flakes, to taste
- Kosher salt as needed for blanching and seasoning
- Lemon wedges, for serving

Preparation

1. Bring a pot of salted water to a boil and blanch the greens and fennel or carrot leaves for 30 seconds to one minute, or until they're tender and taste good to you. (Some greens may take longer to cook than others).
2. Remove the greens to a tray, spreading them out to cool naturally. If your greens are longer than 3 inches, chop them roughly. Squeeze the greens of their water and reserve, it is ok if a little water still clings to some of them, as it will help the pan not dry out as they cook with the oil and onions.
3. Meanwhile, cook the garlic in the oil until it begins to turn golden.
4. Add the onions to the pan and cook for 2 minutes more. Add the paprika, cayenne or red pepper, mint or dill, along with a pinch of salt and cook a minute more. Add the greens, stir to coat with the oil, and adjust the seasoning for salt. Simmer the greens for 5-10 minutes more, when the greens are tender and taste good to you, serve warm or at room temperature, with lemon wedges on the side.

Adding meat

To make the dish as pictured with lamb, take some lamb stew meat, season it with salt and pepper, cover with water and bring to a simmer, covered, until the meat is tender, about 1.5 hours. Cool the lamb, then pat dry. Brown the lamb in oil, seasoning with salt and pepper before serving, and arrange the hot, tender chunks of lamb on the finished dish of greens.

		LUNCH	DINNER
WEEK 1	Day 1	Greek Orzo Salad (pg.2)	Falafel Salad (pg.3)
	Day 2	Lentil Soup (pg.4)	Baked Tilapia with Lemon (pg.5)
	Day 3	Tuna Salad (pg.6)	Lemon Dill Salmon (pg.8)
	Day 4	Quick Hummus Bowls (pg.9)	Moroccan Chickpea Stew (pg.7)
	Day 5	Spanish Paella (pg.11)	Quinoa Stuffed Peppers (pg.10)
	Day 6	Tuscan Soup (pg.13)	Greek Nachos (pg.15)
	Day 7	Mediterranean Couscous (pg.14)	Simple Red Lentil Soup (pg.17)
WEEK 2	Day 1	Best Healthy Pizza (pg.16)	Shakshuka with Feta (pg.19)
	Day 2	Vegetarian Tortellini Soup (pg.18)	Shrimp Marinara (pg.20)
	Day 3	Simple Chickpea Salad (pg.21)	Easy Grain Bowl (pg.30)
	Day 4	Quinoa Tabbouleh (pg.22)	Easy Grilled Tilapia (pg.24)
	Day 5	Asparagus Risotto (pg.32)	Greek Salad (pg.25)
	Day 6	Cozy White Bean Soup (pg.26)	Easy Baked Shrimp (pg.31)
	Day 7	Pasta e Ceci (pg.27)	Lentil Salad with Feta (pg.28)
WEEK 3	Day 1	Baked Eggs and Vegetables (pg.36)	Seared Scallops (pg.29)
	Day 2	Mediterranean Salad (pg.40)	Chickpea Burgers (pg.34)
	Day 3	Fish Sticks (pg.49)	White Bean Salad (pg.44)
	Day 4	Easy Chicken Shawarma (pg.50)	Sautéed Shrimp and Zucchini (pg.61)
	Day 5	Easy Salmon Soup (pg.52)	Ful Mudammas (pg.38)
	Day 6	Cauliflower and Chickpea Stew (pg.43)	Mediterranean Salmon Kabobs (pg.62)
	Day 7	Roasted Tomato Basil Soup (pg.54)	Authentic Falafel (pg.53)
WEEK 4	Day 1	Chicken and Potatoes (pg.60)	Sicilian-Style Fish Stew (pg.66)
	Day 2	Lebanese Rice With Vermicelli (pg.73)	Salmon Burger (pg.56)
	Day 3	Vegetarian Minestrone Soup (pg.74)	Greek Chicken Souvlaki (pg.65)
	Day 4	Mushroom Barley Soup (pg.76)	Garlic Shrimp with Peppers (pg.68)

	Day 5	Tuna Pasta Recipe (pg.77)	Fattoush Salad (pg.87)
	Day 6	Salmon Pita Sandwich (pg.84)	Easy Moroccan Vegetable Tagine (pg.80)
	Day 7	Chicken Thighs with Brussels Sprouts & Gnocchi (pg.81)	Garlic Roasted Salmon & Brussels Sprouts (pg.83)

Made in United States
North Haven, CT
09 March 2023